SCENE DESIGN
RENDERING & MEDIA

"Thirty spokes converge at one hub;
    What is not there makes the wheel useful.
Clay is shaped to form a vessel;
    What is not there makes the vessel useful.
Doors and windows are cut to form a room,
    What is not there makes the room useful.

Therefore, take advantage of what is there,
By making use of what is not."

Lao Tzu
(600-470BC) Chinese philosopher
Drawing by Wenhai Ma

This book is dedicated to my students, colleagues and friends
who inspired and encouraged me.

Scene Design
Rendering & Media

Wenhai Ma

Focus Publishing
R. Pullins Co.
Newburyport, MA

Scene Design Rendering & Media
©2012 Wenhai Ma

Focus Publishing/R. Pullins Company
PO Box 369
Newburyport MA 01950
www.pullins.com

ISBN 13: 978-1-58510-393-5

Printed in the United States of America.

10 9 8 7 6 5 4 3 2 1

1211V

TABLE OF CONTENTS

Chapter 3 Shadow & Light

Chapter 4 Preparing the Sketch

Forward
Steve Arnold

This book is designed to help students and anyone else interested in improving their skill at making finished renderings of scene designs for theater. Anyone studying the craft of scene design will no doubt come across the work of what can be considered the masters of American scene design, people like Robert Edmond Jones, Jo Mielziner, and Donald Oenslager. Not only were their stage designs groundbreaking and brilliant, they were able to present their ideas through artwork that was both evocative and beautiful. Through their sketches and renderings they could show us not only what the sets would look like, but also capture the highly dramatic feeling, lighting and theatricality of a particular moment or scene from a play. This is something we as designers all strive for.

I first met Wenhai when we were both students in the theater department at Carnegie Mellon University and remember realizing I was in the presence of an extremely talented, accomplished designer and artist after seeing his work in our first class. He later helped me by giving me several pointers and I could tell right away he was a natural born teacher. We have stayed in touch over the years as he has progressed in his teaching career and I was extremely happy to hear he was writing a book and including the knowledge and techniques he has learned as a designer and artist. I think a book on this subject is much needed and I truly wish this book had existed when I was a student.

What Wenhai has done in this book is more than what had been suggested by the designer who years ago recommended he put his renderings in a book. He has shown us the process of how he accomplished his final renderings, his methods and techniques, and that is the real value of this book. In each chapter Wenhai has focused on the salient information from various disciplines – drawing, perspective, light and shadow, color mixing, painting, figures, and types of media that are necessary to produce a finished rendering. He then adds his own insights while explaining each aspect in detail and how they relate to each other and why their understanding is necessary to produce a successful finished rendering. Through workshops he explains and shows the various steps in the process of doing a particular rendering from start to finish. I know of no other theater design book that is comparable or is as complete in its handling of the subject.

(Steve Arnold is originally from Seattle Washington and completed his MFA in scenery design for theater at Carnegie Mellon University in Pittsburgh. After designing scenery for small equity waiver theaters he worked in New York City assisting several established Broadway designers. He soon started getting drafting jobs on films and over the years worked his way up the ladder in the Art Department on a number of well known films including **Mississippi Burning**, **The Doors**, **Forrest Gump**, **The Hudsucker Proxy**, *and* **Bugsy** *which won the Oscar for best Art Direction. Subsequently he has been the Art Director on more than 20 feature films including* **Get Shorty**, **Face/Off**, **Unbreakable**, **Spider-Man**, **Van Helsing** *and* **Appaloosa**. *More recently he has begun Production Designing and has designed several independent films including* **Robosapien: Rebooted**, **Deadline** *and* **Em** *which won the Grand Jury Prize at the Seattle International Film Festival and the Criterion Inspiration Award at the Santa Fe Film Festival. He just finished designing the independent neo-noir film* **The Big Bang** *starring Antonio Banderas. Over the years he has had the chance to work with such noted directors as Alan Parker, Oliver Stone, Stephen Frears, Barry Levinson, Terry Gilliam, the Coen Brothers, Steven Soderbergh, Robert Zemeckis, M. Night Shyamalan, Sam Rami and Ang Lee. To date he has been involved in the Art Department on over forty feature films, numerous commercials and several TV shows.)*

Introduction
Wenhai Ma

"I begin with an idea and then it becomes something else."

Pablo Ruiz Picasso (1881 – 1973)
Spanish painter, draughtsman, and sculptor

Back in 1983, while I was a MFA student majoring in Scene & Costume Design at Carnegie Mellon University, I was honorably selected and sent by the University to the Professional League Portfolio Review held at Julliard Music School in New York. My portfolio was very well received by the jury and students.

Amongst the jury members were gathered the most well-established designers, directors, playwrights and critiques in the United States and Canada, such as Ming Cho Lee, Howard Bay, Desmond Healy, Oliver Smith, and many others. They were impressed by my theatre design renderings and sketches. The Artistic Director John Hirsh of the CSSF (Canada Stratford Shakespeare Festival) immediately purchased three of my theatre design renderings for the CSSF's collection.

In front of my display booth, one of the jurors, I believe it was one of the well-known designers, said to me, "These renderings are just amazing. They can simply be put together as a book and get published. So, why don't you do it?" I replied, "Thank you. Maybe I'll do it someday in the future."

That "idea" and "someday" has been in my mind since then but has never been actually established in action.

However, that idea encouraged me to have about a dozen books illustrated and published so far. Nevertheless, I have been thinking about this specific theatre rendering book for quite a while. In the meantime, I have been teaching theatre design rendering at various institutions apart from my regular scene design courses. I have obtained a good idea of what one requires, besides all the common skills, to become a good theatre designer. Furthermore, a good theatre rendering can also be taken as a piece of art, not only illustrating the design concept but also portraying the artistic look and lighting and atmospheric effect.

My theatre design renderings are usually favorably received. This is mainly because of the training I received from the CAD (the Central Academy of Drama) in Beijing and even my being "self-taught" before I went to the CAD. At the CAD, all of the scene design students were required to be in the studio working on still-life, figures, in pencil and oil six days a week from 8:00 am to 12:00 noon. This lasted for four of my BFA years. In addition, each year, we were taken to the countryside to draw and paint on site for four to six weeks. This kind of training style was mainly modeled after Russia, where scene designers and "scenographers" were trained in fine art schools, such as the famous Repin Fine Arts Academy in St. Petersburg. Later, my intensive studies at Carnegie Mellon really refined my skills and artistry. I greatly benefited from both training experiences.

However, before I came to CMU in 1982, right after I graduated from the CAD, I did not get the chance to use watercolor at all; instead I used gouache and oil. When working on my class projects, especially for Barbara and Cletus Anderson's costume design assignments, I decided to try watercolor – mainly because there were so many color plates per assignment and I believed my work would be more efficient if I used watercolor. I picked it up quickly – probably based on my grasp of working with pencil, gouache, and oil. Though each medium has its own nature, characteristics and tricks, the principle of using shadow, light and color theory is the same. Thus, I was able to "produce" fifteen color costume renderings in one night.

During the past twenty-some years of my teaching and design experience, I have realized that there aren't many books on theatre design and there are very few on theatre design rendering all over the world. In my theatre rendering classes I have been giving illustrated handouts with the project briefs to my students. Very often, I illustrate a rendering progression step by step.

I find this is very helpful to the students. I have been saving those handouts with a hope that they could be put together. There is no doubt that such a text book is needed.

I will be very happy if this book may be of some help to young theatre designers when they work in the classroom and in the real world. I'd like to take this opportunity to give thanks to the gentleman designer who encouraged me to "do the book" at Julliard, but I was too busy and a little nervous presenting my portfolio and did not pay attention to who he was.

Acknowledgement

I'd like to acknowledge and give thanks to the following people:
The gentleman scene designer who encouraged me "to put a book together" at Julliard back in 1983; Doris Schneider, Barbara Anderson, Susan Tsu, Steve Arnold, Brian Fizzmorize, Tan Huaixiang, Brant Pope, Ming Cho and my dear family, particularly my wife Yan, my daughter Yaoyao and son-in-law Richard Van As, who have been supporting me all the time.

In memory of my mentors and friends: Cletus Anderson, Elden Elder and Fred Youens.

1

THE STUDIO & TOOLS

"First of all, respect your paper!"

J. M. W. Turner (1775 – 1851)
English Romantic landscape painter, watercolorist and printmaker.

The Studio

A theatre designer's working environment, the studio or work space, is not like that of most other office-based professions. The Studio can be "ideal" — fully-equipped and fully-furnished. The designer is surrounded by his/her design hand tools including paints, brushes, pencils pens, rulers, x-acto knives, swinging lamps; and equipment such as light boxes, cutting tables, spray booths and storage space for models and sketches. It is for these reasons that many designers eventually decide to find premises away from their living environment.

Here is a picture showing such a studio with all the furnishings and equipment. However, I believe that most of the students and young designers will not have such luxury for a while. I myself used to work in spaces with only the very minimum and most-needed supplies around me.

Figure 1-1. *A fully-equipped and furnished design studio. Rendering by Wenhai Ma, Photoshop over pencil sketch.*

Figure 1- 2. *A work station with the most-needed supplies: a large desk and a chair (not included in the figure), pencil sketch taped on drawing board, a watercolor pan set, a porcelain watercolor palette, two water containers, a hair dryer, three brushes: one 3" flat soft brush, one No. 2 round watercolor brush, one Chinese soft "Medium White Cloud" brush, a paper towel, the pencil shadow and light study sketch and the Photoshop-aided color study sketch. Above the table there are two desk top white fluorescent lights. Photoshop sketch by Wenhai Ma.*

The Furniture, Basic Equipments and Tools

Below is a list of the tools I use when I work on renderings. I tend to keep things simple.

Drafting table & chair. An adjustable drafting table sized around 43" W x 24" D x 31.5" H inches is efficient and handy. On top of it I tend to put a drawing board with my sketch taped on it so it is easier for me to turn it around when I need to. Facing the sketch on the right angle helps read and deal with the lines and perspective well. See figures below.

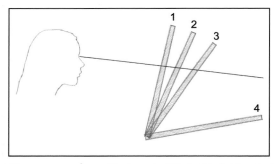 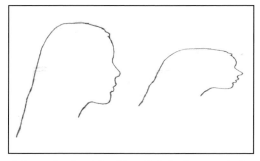

Figures 1-3 and 1-4. *The viewer should look at the sketch on the drawing board at an angle such as 1, 2 and 3, particularly when preparing the sketch. Position 4 is actually a distorted angle, as shown in Figure 1-4, the profile on the right.*

Light: Unless there is good natural light source in your studio that allows you to read colors accurately, you may like to put a "True Color Light" by your table. Such light fixtures are usually used by painters and graphic designers because the light is close to natural light. Otherwise, fluorescent light can be used as an alternative. Ideally there is a light on each side of your table, in order to get even light without shadows being cast.

Light table: It is used for transferring the sketch onto watercolor paper.

Hair dryer: It is used to help your watercolor paper dry faster.

Art Supplies & Materials for Watercolor

I'd like to start with watercolor because this is the medium I have been using most in the past twenty-five years for my scenic and costume renderings.

Pencils

2H, HB. A 2H drawing pencil is good for transferring a line sketch to watercolor paper. Because of the light line weight, it allows you to have the lines refined and reinforced by using an HB pencil after. I never take the traced lines as the final look because they are usually mechanical and lack vitality.

I tend to keep some of the "sketchy" pencil strokes on my renderings even though I usually use India ink to go over and reinforce the lines. Some sketchy lines help build the three-dimensionality and provide an atmospheric quality. I also sometimes use a mechanical pencil with an HB lead for this step. I tend to sharpen my pencils with an X-acto knife instead of a pencil sharpener for I find it is easier to sharpen the lead with better control.

Waterproof Ink and Pens

I use a kind of waterproof ink also called "India ink". I personally like to use sepia or brown because it is a mixture of the three primary colors. It is the color between the cool color category and the warm color category so it goes well with either of the two. Certainly you may use black or blue. Any of the three colors should work well. Depending on what kind of pen you use, you may get bottled ink with a wide opening for your graphic pens to dip the ink. Or, you may get bottled ink for fountain pens.

If you like to ink your sketch with waterproof ink, I recommend two pens: a graphic dip pen and a refillable fountain pen. The dip pen nib I use is size 2B but it can be different depending on the line weight you desire. The one I use is a 0.3, 1x0 "TG 1-S Faber-Castell" fountain technical pen — a drawing pen with cartridge or refillable reservoir. You may also get a set with different sizes for various line weights.

Figure 1-5. *Paint, ink, brushes and palette. Photoshop-aided photo by Wenhai Ma.*

Figure 1-6. *Drawing pencils.*

Figures 1-7 and 1-8. *Ink and pens. Photoshop-aided photo by Wenhai Ma.*

Paper

Watercolor paper comes in three surfaces. The first is rough, which has a textured surface. The second is hot-pressed, which has a fine-grained, smooth surface, and the third is cold-pressed, which has a slightly textured surface and is the most favorable kind for many watercolorists. The thickness of paper is indicated by its weight. The standard machine weights are 190 gsm (90 lb), 300 gsm (140 lb), 356 gsm (260 lb), and 638 gsm (300 lb). Paper less than 356 gsm (260 lb) should be stretched before use, otherwise it's likely to warp.

It is very important to use high-quality watercolor paper. I tend to use Arches Watercolor paper, cold press/Grain Fin, 140 lb, 260 lb, and 300 lb for my renderings. For practice purpose, you may start with paper from a watercolor pad which is relatively cheap and convenient. When you have better control of water coloring, I highly recommend you use high-quality individual watercolor paper sheets, trimmed to the desired sizes for your renderings. You may not get the desired watercolor effect by using cheap paper.

Figure 1-9. *Illustration by Wenhai Ma. Note most of the lines were done with a graphic dip pen. The advantage of a dip pen is that the line weight can be controlled by the pressure you apply when you draw.*

Watercolor paper is usually white, but it need not be. A variety of cool and warm tints are available. High-quality acid-free paper is best for renderings that you wish to keep for good because it will not be yellowed by age. Watercolor paper differs from manufacturer to manufacturer so experiment not only with the different kinds of paper but also with various brands of paper. You might like to stay with a couple of particular kinds and brands for some time!

Paint

Watercolor paint can be bought either in tubes or in pans and it comes in different brands and various qualities. I usually use Winsor & Newton or Holbein Artists' Water Color. Unlike other types of paint such as oil, acrylic and gouache, watercolor paint can be considered an economic medium because the density of colors is determined by water — it lasts. Therefore, I highly recommend you use high-quality watercolor paint.

The following colors are highly recommended.
- Ivory Black, or Lamp Black
- Prussian Blue, or Phthalocyanine Blue
- Scarlet, or Cadmium Red
- Lemon Yellow, or Cadmium Yellow
- Crimson Lake, or Rose Madder Alizarin
- Green Deep, or Viridian Hue
- Van Dyke Brown, or Burnt Umber
- Watercolor white, or gouache white.

Watercolor is reusable, unlike acrylic, so it is OK if you leave paint on your palette. The paint can be used again even if it gets dried. Paint comes in tubes or pans (small blocks). Pans are usually cheaper and more easily accessible, but tend to dry out. They are ideal for small areas of color and watercolor sketching. Paint in tubes has to be squeezed onto a palette. They are easier to use for large areas of color. There's a big difference between student and professional

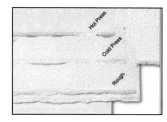

Figure 1-10. *Watercolor paper with different weights and surfaces. Photoshop-aided photo by Wenhai Ma.*

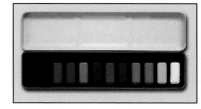

Figure 1-11. *A watercolor set with pans. Photoshop-aided photo by Wenhai Ma.*

paints. I'd rather buy smaller amounts of high-quality paint in tubes than large amounts of cheap, low-quality paint in a pan set.

You may use a watercolor set with pans though you will need to make sure that you have the three primary colors or colors close to them. Very often, in watercolor sets, the Primary Red and Primary Yellow are good but the blue is usually odd – it tends to be more like Cobalt Blue instead. You must have a blue that is close to Prussian Blue or Phthalocyanine Blue. I consider these as "Primary Blues" and there is no way to obtain such colors by mixing whatever colors you have! I'd also recommend you get a Van Dyke Brown. I find this color is very useful for theatre design renderings, since it is a color that sits in between the warm color category and the cool color category. You may get these colors in individual tubes.

When watercolor paint in a tube has dried hard, you may cut it open to the paint, and then use it like you would for a pan or a paint block. That is, gently rub a wet brush onto the dried paint making it dissolve into the water. If the paint has thickened but can still be coaxed out of the tube, squeeze or scrape it onto a palette. It will dry slowly on the palette, but remain usable like a watercolor pan. Unlike acrylics, watercolor paint remains water-soluble when dry, so you can always "reactivate" it with a wet brush.

Brushes

Watercolor brushes: #4; #8; I like to use round brushes with soft bristles. I even like to use Chinese watercolor brushes such as the "Medium White Cloud", with goat bristles. I also like to use the flat oriental brush with soft goat bristles called "FLT SHT HN" that comes in different sizes. I recommend the 3". Such brushes are used for wetting the paper and, occasionally, for laying out the atmospheric backgrounds in the first couple of steps. Such brushes are also used for varnishing. The Japanese Holbein Hake Brush with soft, white goat bristles can be an option. Or, a Japanese Yasutomo Flat Hake Brush, either 2-1/2" or 3-1/4" will work suitably well.

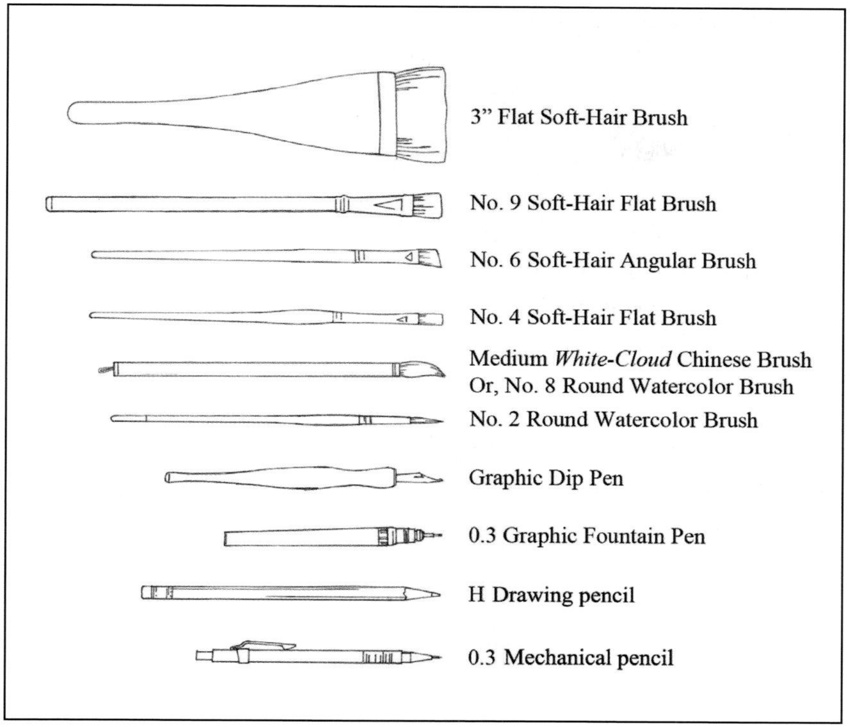
3" Flat Soft-Hair Brush
No. 9 Soft-Hair Flat Brush
No. 6 Soft-Hair Angular Brush
No. 4 Soft-Hair Flat Brush
Medium *White-Cloud* Chinese Brush
Or, No. 8 Round Watercolor Brush
No. 2 Round Watercolor Brush
Graphic Dip Pen
0.3 Graphic Fountain Pen
H Drawing pencil
0.3 Mechanical pencil

Figure 1-12. *A set of brushes, pencils and pens I usually use for renderings. Sketch by Wenhai Ma.*

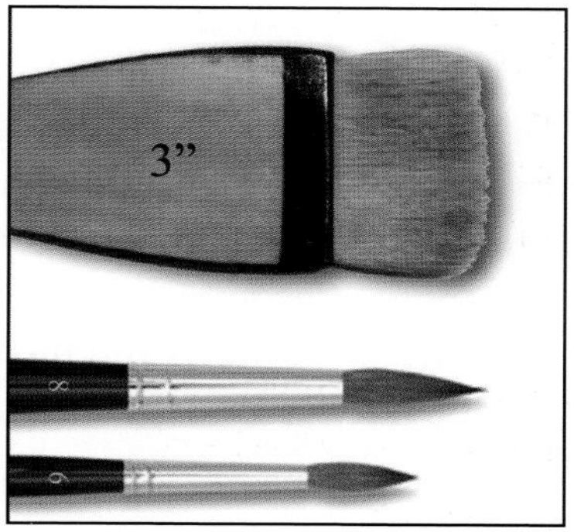
3"

Figure 1-13. *If there is a limit, these three brushes are enough for most of my theatre design renderings: a 3" flat brush, a No. 8 round watercolor brush and a No. 2 round watercolor brush. Photoshop-aided photo by Wenhai Ma.*

For small sized renderings around 4" x 6" or smaller, the 3" flat brush may not be needed. You may use a regular round #4 watercolor brush instead. Sable brushes are considered the ultimate in watercolor brushes because of the fine point the hairs reach, their ability to spring back into shape, and the amount of paint they hold. Less expensive options are brushes with a mixture of sable and synthetic hairs or 100% synthetic brushes.

Palettes

I mostly utilize the regular palette that comes with watercolor paint in pans. In addition, I use a porcelain watercolor palette or a small dish for preparing large watercolor washes for the background in the first couple of steps. I like to have enough color mixed and prepared so that area will stay consistent in color and color density. A large flat plastic or china dinner plate may also be an alternative.

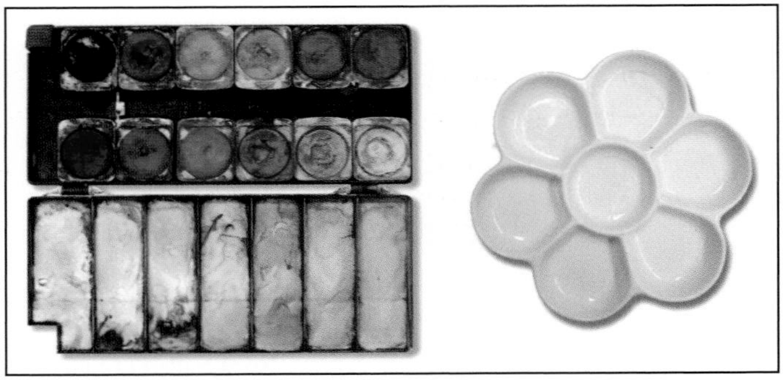

Tracing Paper

I find that tracing paper is very useful for sketching and editing the images. I occasionally use transparent paper (though it is not as widely available nowadays) or transparencies for the same purpose.

Drawing Board

I like to tape my inked sketch (on watercolor paper) on a wooden drawing board for coloring. Such a drawing board can be a two-sided hollow-core artist drawing board or a piece of plywood for wood block printing, ideally made of white birch wood for it absorbs water well. I do not recommend any plastic board or plastic-coated board for this purpose. I recommend that such a drawing board be 2" wider than the rendering on each side so it allows you the extra room for taping.

Figures 1-14. *The palettes I have been using for most of my renderings. Photo by Wenhai Ma.*

Figure 1-15. *Tracing paper. Photo by Wenhai Ma.*

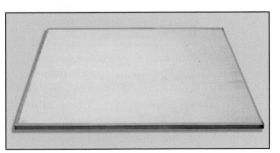

Figure 1-16. *A wooden drawing board. Photo by Wenhai Ma.*

Masking Tape and Gummed Tape

I recommend 1" masking tape and gummed tape. I always tape my sketch on the drawing board and find it very handy when I color and sketch. Be sure not to use old masking tape or tape that has been exposed to heat for any length of time as it may be very sticky and hard to peel off when your rendering is finished.

Water Containers

This can be a glass or a jar. I like to use a jar that is wide enough for the 3" wide FLT SHT HN brush. Very often, I keep two water containers when rendering: one of them is for the FLT SHT HN brush with clean water, and the other for regular use. I also recommend clear water containers because it is easier to check the water level when you dip your brush in and also easier for you to tell when the water gets too dirty and needs to be replaced.

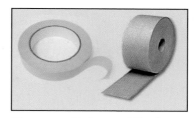

Figure 1-17. *Masking tape (1") and gummed brown tape. Photo by Wenhai Ma.*

Figure 1-18. *Water containers. Photo by Wenhai Ma.*

Paper Towels

Kitchen paper towels are good enough. When cleaning your brush, you may rinse it in water, and then soak the water out on the towel. You may also use a paper towel to control the water quantity in the brush. Occasionally, when you have an "accident", say you've dropped paint on the paper accidentally, you may use a paper towel to dip it out. Always keep some paper towels handy around you!

Figure 1-19. *Kitchen paper towels. Photo by Wenhai Ma.*

2

PERSPECTIVE

"Perspective is the rein and rudder of painting."
"The most praiseworthy form of painting is the one that most resembles what it imitates."

Leonardo da Vinci (1452-1519)
Italian polymath: painter, sculptor, architect, musician, scientist, mathematician, engineer, inventor, anatomist, geologist, cartographer, botanist and writer.

Most of the time, perspective is thought to be very hard to grasp and confusing to deal with. In fact it is not really always that way. It can be a fun thing – like problem solving or putting the puzzle pieces together! It's very satisfying when the perspective in your sketch looks good and accurate. A sketch with the correct perspective is preferable because it shows the exact look of your design on the stage. It makes you confident with your design.

The word "perspective" came from the ancient Latin word *perspicere* meaning "to look through." It is the way in which objects appear to the eye based on their spatial attributes. The perspective method was gradually developed through history. The artwork done before the Renaissance, although beautiful, seems awkward and primitive to our eyes because the artists did not understand the methods of linear perspective at that time.

Perspective was not really well known or developed till the Italian Renaissance times. Italian artists invented linear perspective and aerial perspective. These perspective methods make a flat surface appear to have three dimensions and an illusion of distance and space. Italian architect Brunelleschi made the great discovery of "the Center Perspective Method". Italian artist and architect Leon Battista Alberti (1404 – 1474) codified the basic geometry so that linear perspective became mathematically coherent and related to the spectator. *Figures 2-1, 2-2, and 2-3* show Albert Dürer (1471 – 1528, German painter, printmaker and theorist) studying perspective with the perspective machines he invented.

Figures 2-1. *Wenhai Ma's adaptation of woodcut illustration by* Dürer. *He shows how the reclining women may be drawn in perspective by use of a reticulated net set up between artist and subject. The artist can simply transfer the image as seen in the small units that divide the net onto a piece of paper with corresponding squares.*

Figures 2-2 and 2-3. *Wenhai Ma's adaptation of woodcut illustrations by Dürer. He demonstrates how a painter, by using an eyepiece, can sight his subjects and draw in the subjects' contours onto a piece of glass.*

To understand perspective, one should first understand the HL (horizon line) and the VP (vanishing point) and how the lines vanish. An efficient and easy way to start is to take a bunch of photographs of architecture and use your ruler and pen to find out the horizon line and the vanishing point(s) by lining up certain lines, as shown in *Figure 2-5*. This is very similar to Dürer's demonstration of how a painter, by using an eyepiece, can sight his subjects and draw in the subjects' contours onto a piece of glass.

Terms and Definitions

HL — The Horizon Line: Also known as the "Eye Level Line". The actual horizon is where the earth (or ocean) meets the sky. The HL is an imaginary line where the earth meets the sky without objects, hills or valleys in the way. This is also called "eye level". This line is drawn across the page and represents the eye level of the viewer. The height of the HL changes depending on the viewer's height. This changes the view of the subject.

VP —The Vanishing Point: The VP is a point at which parallel lines receding into space appear to meet.

Figure 2-4. *Satire on False Perspective, engraving by William Hogarth (English artist, 1697-1764) 1754. His illustration shows a scene that portrays deliberate examples of confused and misplaced perspective effects. Look at the boxed segments in the picture and see what errors you can find. Photoshop-edited by Wenhai Ma.*

OP – The Observation Point: The OP is a point between the observer's eyes going to the HL. In one-point perspective, it is also the VPC.

VPC – The Vanishing Point Center: The VPC is a point at which all the parallel lines on each side of the objects receding into space appear to meet. It is actually the observation point on the horizon line.

PP – The Picture Plane: The picture plane is the actual surface of a drawing or painting.

Vertical – In perspective terms a vertical line is perpendicular to the horizon line. A vertical line is "standing up".

Horizontal – In perspective terms a horizontal line is parallel to the horizon line. A horizontal line is "lying down".

Perpendicular – Perpendicular means connecting at a right angle or 90-degree angle. Absolute vertical and absolute horizontal lines are perpendicular.

Parallel – Parallel lines are lines that are always the same distance from each other. They never meet.

Foreshortening – The term foreshortening refers to the fact that although things are the same size in reality, such as a line of fence posts, floor tiles, or two arms and legs, they appear to be smaller when farther away, and larger when up close.

Receding – Moving away from the viewer. (Opposite - Advancing.)

Diminishing Forms – Refers to the apparent size of objects and how they become smaller when in the distance.

Figure 2-5. *Note the buildings vanish to the VP on the HL. The HL, in this scene, is actually the "line" separating the sky and the sea in distance. Photoshop sketch by Wenhai Ma.*

Ground line – The bottom of the picture plane.

Line of Sight – An imaginary line traveling from the eye of the spectator to infinity.

Converging lines – Parallel lines that come together towards a single vanishing point.

Orthogonal lines – Imaginary or lightly drawn guidelines in a perspective drawing. They are usually the parallel lines that converge onto the horizon line.

Plane – Any flat surface such as a wall, floor, meadow, or table top is a plane.

Linear Perspective – Using perspective is simply a way of using lines based on strict rules of geometry that gives the illusion of depth and distance. These rules were designed to help you draw three-dimensional objects on a flat surface.

The following figures will further help you understand the vocabulary.

Figure 2-6 shows the following additional terms:
GP – Ground Plan
VP – View Plane
VA – Visual Angle
OL – Observation Line
PP – Picture Plane
OH – Observation Height
CP – Center Point
VD – Visual Distance
NVZ – Normal Visual Zone

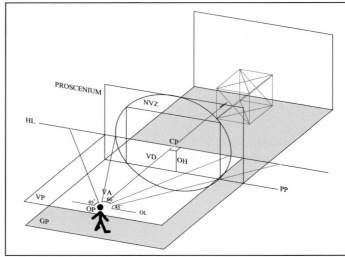

Figure 2-6. *Photoshop sketch by Wenhai Ma.*

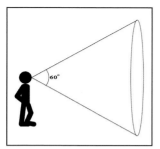

Figure 2-7. *The visual cone. The human's normal visual zone is a 60 degree angle cone. Photoshop sketch by Wenhai Ma.*

Figure 2-8. *The HL (the horizon line) in this picture is the imaginary line where the sky meets the ocean. It is also the viewer's eye level. Photoshop sketch by Wenhai Ma.*

Changing the location of the vanishing point or raising and lowering the eye level will affect perspective.

One-Point Perspective

One-point perspective is a type of linear perspective where the sides of the object that are facing the viewer are parallel to the picture plane and the parallel lines that recede from the viewer converge to a single vanishing point. One-point perspective method is typically used for pictures with roads, light poles and railroad tracks.

The principal surface of an object is parallel to the picture plane and to the observation point. The remaining structure of the object is perpendicular to the picture plane. For this reason, one-point perspective is also called parallel perspective. One of the most common uses of one-point perspective is in interior architectural illustrations.

One-point or parallel perspective places two principal edges (height and width) of one surface of an object parallel to the picture plane. Height and width have no vanishing point and appear in true length since they are parallel to the picture plane. Only the depth dimension must be put in perspective, and this requires one vanishing point. The observation point is in front and parallel to the object and the vanishing point is directly behind.

Figure 2-9. *Clearly we see the HL and the VPC in this alleyway picture. Photo by Wenhai Ma*

Figure 2-10. The Last Supper *by Leonardo da Vinci. This is a typical one-point perspective. Note that the VPC is on Jesus' face.*

Figure 2-11. The School of Athens *(1518) by Raffaello Sanzio (1483-1520). A fine example of architectural perspective with a central vanishing point.*

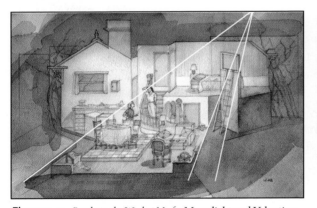

Figure 2-12. *Rendering by Wenhai Ma for* Moonlight and Valentino, *watercolor on paper, 13"x7 ½", 1990. Note that I intentionally set the HL higher than usual so the scenic elements in the design were shown better.*

Figure 2-13. *Rendering by Wenhai Ma for* A Doll's House, *watercolor, gouache and white pencil on mat board, 19" x 9", 1982.*

Freehand One-Point Perspective

Now the question is how to start a freehand one-point perspective drawing. Let's start with boxes and develop them into furniture.

Developing Furniture from Boxes

All objects can be simplified into boxes, or sometimes cylinders. This method may help you understand perspective better. I can assure you that no matter how complicated the perspective may appear to be, things can be figured out by breaking them down into boxes.

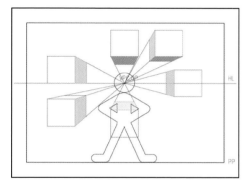
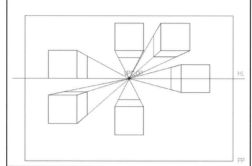

Figures 2-14 and 2-15. *One-Point Perspective. Photoshop sketch by Wenhai Ma.*

Figure 2-16. *One-Point Perspective: Houses can be started as "boxes". Photo by Wenhai Ma.*

The front view, or elevation of each box, or cube, can be simply obtained as an elevation, as in technical drafting – a square or a rectangle. Place the HL on a desirable height and determine the vanishing point, or the observation point.

Imagine the side(s) of the box that are seen in depth. Draw a straight line from each corner of the side(s) in depth to the VPC. Determine the depth of the box or cube by "eyeballing it". It is a way to train your observation ability and judgment comprehension. I'll explain an accurate way to determine the depth in the Grid Perspective Method section.

At this moment, you may check and figure out the depth based on your own sense and judgment and your perspective should look pretty good. In *Figure 2-17,* the sofa on the left looks too deep while the sofa on the right looks correct. In *Figure 2-18,* the legs of the table on the left look too fat. The legs of the table on the right look a lot better. So, use your own common sense to determine the depth.

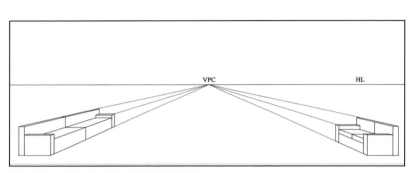

Figure 2-17. *AutoCAD sketch by Shang Yan Liang.*

Figure 2-18. *AutoCAD sketch by Shang Yan Liang.*

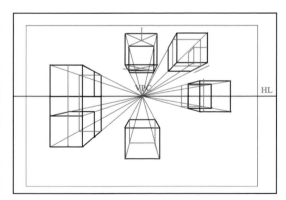

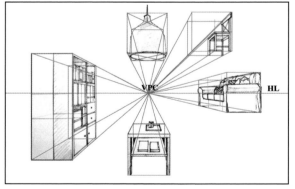

Figures 2-19 and 2-20. *Developing Furniture from Boxes. Note I developed the bookcase from two boxes on the left but narrowed the width. I scaled down the box on the upper right to make the proportions of the chair look right. The light fixture is enormously large, but the idea is to show you how I developed the cylinder from a box. You may use the same method developing your set pieces. Sketches by Wenhai Ma.*

Developing a Set from Boxes

You may use the same method developing a set design elevation. Simply start with a box for the stage, and then add the set pieces, starting them as boxes.

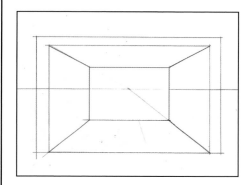
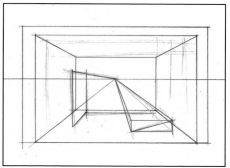
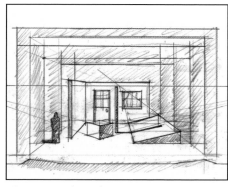
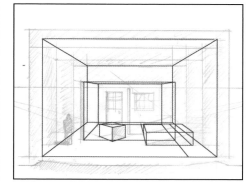

Figures 2-21 through 2-24. *Developing a set from boxes. Note* Figure 2-24 *shows how the scenic elements are 'boxed'. Sketches by Wenhai Ma.*

Two-Point Perspective

Two-point perspective is a type of linear perspective where the sides of the object that face the viewer are at an angle to the picture plane and the parallel lines that recede from the viewer converge to two vanishing points.

Two-point perspective can be used to draw the same objects as one-point perspective, rotated: looking at the corner of a house, or looking at two forked roads shrink into the distance, for example. One point represents one set of parallel lines; the other point represents the other set. Looking at a house from the corner, one wall would recede towards one vanishing point and the other wall would recede towards the opposite vanishing point.

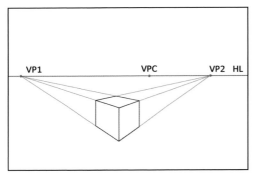

Figure 2-25. *Two-Point Perspective: When a box is placed not in parallel with the picture plane, the sides of the box do not vanish on the VPC but on the same HL. AutoCAD sketch by Shang Yan Liang.*

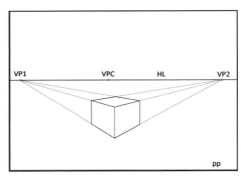 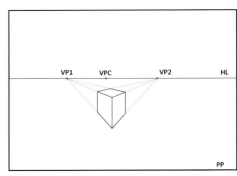

Figures 2-26 and 2-27. *The boxes look awkward in the two drawings: the 2 VPs are either too far apart, or too close. AutoCAD sketches by Shang Yan Liang.*

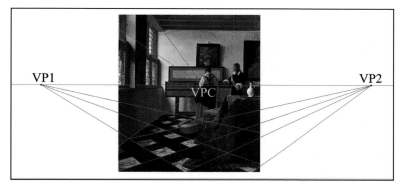

Figure 2-28. *The Music Lesson, by Johannes Vermeer, 1662-1665, Oil on canvas, 74.6 x 64.1 cm. Royal Collection, St. James' Palace, London. This is a fine example of one-point perspective for the house and two-point perspective for the tiles on the floor.*

Figure 2-29. *Note this illustration by Wenhai Ma for* Monkey King Wreaks Havoc in Heaven *(Pan Asian Publications, 2000) involves two vanishing points on the same HL.*

Three-Point Perspective

Three-Point Perspective is a type of linear perspective where the sides of the object that face the viewer are at an angle to the picture plane and the parallel lines that recede from the viewer converge to three vanishing points.

A third point can come into play in perspective, but only when dealing with extreme heights or lows. Tall buildings are one example. In the case of looking down at a tall building (bird's eye view) the edges of the building will not only recede to the two vanishing points (if looking at corner), but there will be an downward recession to a vanishing point. This vanishing point is always directly in front of the viewer at a 90 degree angle to the horizon line. Looking up at an object in three point perspective is referred to as a "worm's eye view".

In three-point perspective, every right-angle line in the drawing will eventually converge on one of three perspective points. This can look distorted if the vanishing points are too close together, but if they are far enough apart, three-point perspective is the most accurate way of drawing the world around you in three dimensions.

Three-point perspective is probably the most challenging of all.

The Third VP in the Ground, a Bird's Eye View

Imagine when you look down from an airplane flying over a big city with lots of skyscrapers, as seen in *Figure 2-30*. The skyscrapers, or "boxes", have three vanishing points – with VP1 and VP2 sharing the same HL while the VP3 is below.

The vertical lines of the buildings will be a downward recession to a vanishing point in the ground. This is usually called a "bird's-eye view".

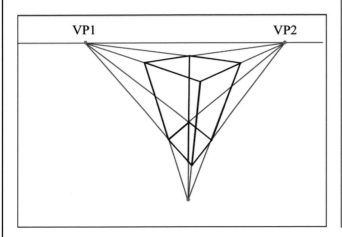

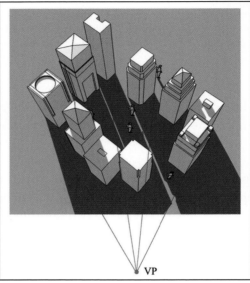

Figures 2-30 and 2-31. *Note that the vertical lines of the buildings vanish at the same VP in the ground, while the horizontal lines of the buildings vanish on each side. AutoCAD, Photoshop and Sketch-Up sketches by Wenhai Ma.*

The Third VP in the Sky, a Worm's Eye View

Imagine you are looking at the high-rises in Time Square, New York City as seen in *Figures 2-33.* You'll see the vertical lines of the buildings, or "boxes" have three vanishing points – with VP1 and VP2 sharing the same HL while the VP3 is above. The vertical lines of the buildings will be an upward recession to a vanishing point in the sky. This is the "worm's-eye view".

Three-point perspective is usually seen on backdrops or projections.

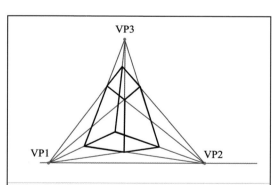

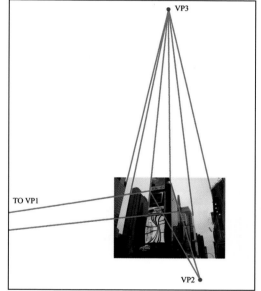

Figures 2-32 though 2-34. *Note that the vertical lines vanish at the same VP in the sky, while the horizontal lines vanish on each side on the HL. AutoCAD and Photoshop sketches by Wenhai Ma.*

Perspective for Ramps and Raked Platforms

Scene designers usually love to put ramps and raked platforms on the stage.

The method of dealing with the perspective for ramps and raked platforms is very similar to what is explained in the previous section – the three-point perspective method. See the following figures and explanations.

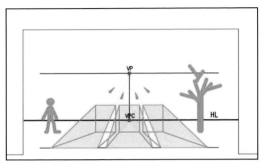
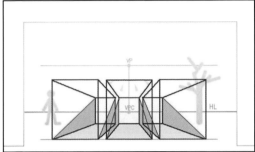

Figures 2-35 and 2-36. *This figure involves the one-point and the three-point perspective methods. Imagine the three ramps as boxes. The boxes share one VP on the HL. Then trim them into ramps as shown in* **Figure 36.** *Note that the three ramp tops share a vanishing point above the HL. Though this drawing has two vanishing points, it is not a two-point perspective but a mixture of one-point and three-point, because VP3 is above the HL, in the sky. Photoshop sketch by Wenhai Ma.*

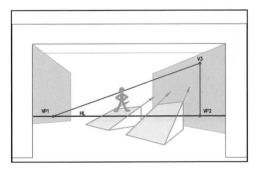
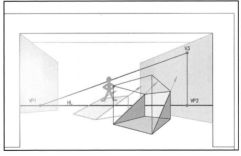

Figures 2-37 and 2-38. *These two figures show how ramps are created from boxes. The drawings involves the two-point perspective and three-point perspective methods.*

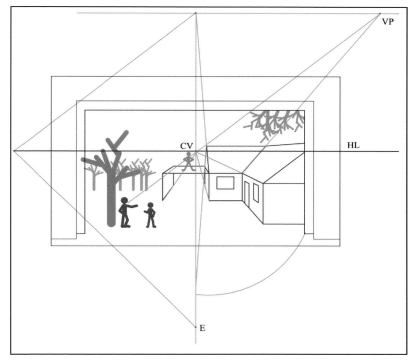

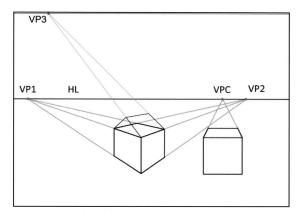

Figure 2-40. *Though this is a simple picture with two boxes only, it involves the one-point, two-point and three-point perspective methods. Note the box on the right is a typical one-point perspective with the VPC, or the OP, where the observer's eyes are, while the box on the left has two vanishing points sharing the same HL with the box on the right. The roof has a VP in the sky. Most of the settings we design are actually dealing with these 2 "boxes" plus a "roof". AutoCAD sketch by Shang Yan Liang.*

Figure 2-39. *This figure shows an exterior setting with two houses, a raised level, probably a carport, and some trees. Note the roofs have their own VPs, while the houses share a VPC. So, this picture involves the one-perspective method and the three-point perspective method, for the VP is in the sky. Photoshop sketch by Wenhai Ma.*

On the stage, the scenic elements are placed in various positions, on different levels and at different angles. No matter how complicated it might be, the boxes and roof in *Figure 2-40* may help you figure things out.

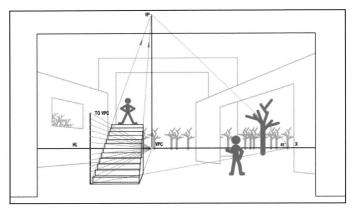

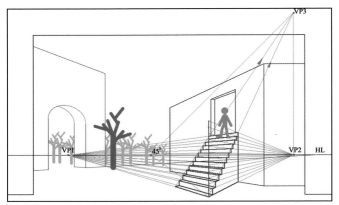

Figure 2-41. *This figure includes a staircase which involves a "ramp" – if you imagine the steps forming it. The "ramp" has its VP3 in the sky, like the roof of the house shown in* Figure 2-33. *The base of the staircase and each step goes to the one-point perspective method. This picture also uses the two-point perspective method for the diagonal scenic units – the one on stage left with an opening and the one on stage right with a window. Each of the units has its own VP, but they share the same HL. The base of the staircase vanishes on the VPC on the HL; so do the steps. The roof in* Figure 2-40 *may help explain the "ramp" in this figure.*

Figure 2-42. *This figure is a typical three-point perspective. The staircase forms a "ramp". The "ramp" has a vanishing point in the sky (VP3). The base of the ramp and each step have two vanishing points, on the same HL. The two wall units use the two-perspective method. The one on stage left, with the staircase attached shares the VPs with the base of staircase and the steps. The wall unit on stage right has its own VPs on the same HL. The roof in* Figure 2-40 *may help explain the "ramp" in this figure.*

Additional Hints

There is *one* HL in the picture.

There is *one* VPC in the picture though there are might be more than one VP.

The pictures may involve objects with their sides vanishing at the VPC on the HL; which means this is "one-point perspective". In the meantime, there are objects vanishing not at the VPC but on the *same* HL. Furthermore there are objects vanishing somewhere else – into the sky, or into the ground.

Most of the VPs are on the HL, except ramps, roofs and raked surfaces.

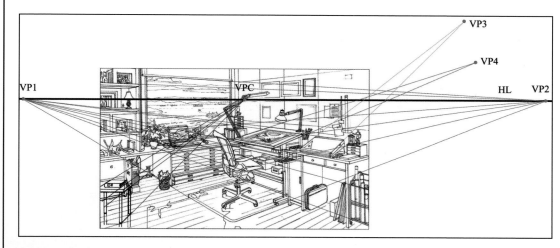

Figure 2-43. *Note that most of the objects we see in this drawing follow the two-point perspective method, but the stool on the lower left and the book on top of it follow the one-point perspective method. In other words any rectilinear object with one side parallel to the picture plane can be drawn using the one-point perspective method. For the top of the drafting table and the top of the light box, since they are tilted like the raked platforms we see on stage, each of the tops has two VPs, one sharing the same VP with the other objects in the room and the others somewhere above the HL in the sky, depending the degree of the angle. Sketch by Wenhai Ma.*

Figure 2-44. *Illustration by Wenhai Ma for* Red Means Good Fortune *(Viking, 1994.) It is an old street scene in San Francisco. Note that the houses along the street vanish on the true HL while the hilly street vanishes somewhere into the sky because it is raked.*

Zero-Point Perspective

Due to the fact that vanishing points exist only when parallel lines are present in the scene, a perspective without any vanishing points ("zero-point" perspective) occurs if the viewer is observing a nonlinear scene. The most common example of a nonlinear scene is a natural scene (e.g., a mountain range) which frequently does not contain any parallel lines. A perspective without vanishing points can still create a sense of "depth," as is clearly apparent in a photograph of a mountain range (more distant mountains have smaller-scale features).

Aerial Perspective

Aerial perspective refers to changes caused by distance and atmospheric conditions.

Figure 2-45. *Photograph by Wenhai Ma. Though there is no linear perspective involved in the scene, it has a sense of depth because the mountains and trees get smaller in scale. In the meantime, because the air absorbs the warm colors and the density of the image, the distant mountains get lighter and bluer. This can also be referred to as aerial perspective, or color perspective.*

Usually color perspective is referred in landscape painting, because greater distances and spatial problems are encountered in these subjects, though it also takes an important role in figures and portraits. We usually see the background behind the figures or portraits, as we see in Leonardo da Vinci's *Mona Lisa*.

When we work on a scene design rendering, besides linear perspective, we should also have a good understanding of color perspective or what was called aerial perspective — meaning everything pertaining to the air and the atmosphere. The atmosphere scatters light. It also plays a role in our depth perception. We usually see the sky and the ocean as blue, the trees as green, and the flowers as red, pink, white or yellow. The short or blue wavelengths of light are most easily scattered every which way by the particles in the atmosphere, which is why the sky and ocean look blue, although scattering does occur to some extent for other wavelengths of light.

Figure 2-46. *Leonardo da Vinci's* Mona Lisa, *tempera on cottonwood, 1503–1505, Musée du Louvre*

Look at the landscape we see through a window. Look at the trees. The trees close to us look green, as what our perception is. We know green is a mixture of yellow and blue. However, the trees in the distance look a lot lighter in value and such green seems to have less yellow in it. The trees very far away from us covering the mountains do not look green but saturated and shifting towards the background color which is usually blue. This is color perspective. The blues are thinned and discolored by the air and the distance.

Aerial perspective refers to the technique of creating an illusion of depth by depicting distant objects as paler, less detailed, and usually bluer than near objects.

Leonardo da Vinci was the first of a few who paid good attention not only to linear perspective but also color perspective. Examine the picture of Mona Lisa, especially compare the appearance of the foreground to the portion of the rim of the mountains in the distance. The texture on the near side is clear, sharp, and tinged with warm hues. The far rim is less distinct, and less distinct than can be accounted for just because it is farther away; it has a decidedly bluish cast.

Colors do change according to distance. Mountains, hills and objects in the distance are not only smaller than similar objects closer to us, but they are also bluer. Though some very bright hues still seem bright in the distance they are a lot lighter and weaker.

Figures 2-47 and 2-48. *These two photographs show how the green colors are reduced in perspective. The mountains look a lot bluer in distance. Photos by Wenhai Ma.*

Weather also affects colors. In a rainy or misty day all colors become grayer and the objects we see seem more layered. This is very similar to the fog or dry ice we use for certain effects on stage in the theatre.

Figures 2-49 and 2-50. *Note how the mist affects the colors and layers the objects. Photo and Photoshop sketch by Wenhai Ma.*

Figure 2-51 is a fine example of aerial perspective depicted by Joseph Mallord William Turner.

Figure 2-51. The Red Rigi, *Joseph William Mallord Turner, National Gallery of Victoria, Melbourne, Australia.*

Shadow Perspective

When you walk in the street in a sunny day and pay attention to the shadows on houses cast by trees, street light poles, neighboring houses, etc, you may enjoy the beauty that the sunshine creates. In the theatre, we see light and shadows on the stage all the time. Stage light tells the story of time, the season, the region, the mood, the drama, the color, the texture and the music. As we say, lighting is the soul of the setting. It is the same in art work and in theatre design renderings. I always pay a great attention to shadow and light when I render.

I always prepare a pencil sketch before coloring. Such a sketch can be very small and quick – around 5"x7" or even smaller. It is an efficient way to plan the atmospheric mood, the shadow and light arrangement I would like for the rendering.

Understanding the basic shadow perspective principles may help you better illustrate your scene – the rendering. Because your rendering is not just a sheet of paper with a group of drafted and colored scenic elements, but rather the general artistic atmospheric look of the stage picture, you therefore must show certain lighting effect and apply shadows cast by the scenic elements and the actors.

Though dealing with shadow perspective can be very tricky, it is similar to how we deal with the perspective for the "boxes". To create believable shadows one must first draw the objects as transparent. This is because you will need to know where the back corners are in order to finish a shadow which may disappear behind the object.

You may need to understand a few terms and the concept first:

LS – The light source: The light source in nature is the sun, while on the stage, it is the artificial lights.

VL – The vertical line: It descends directly from the light source or light vanishing point until it intersects with the surface where the shadow is being cast.

SVP — The shadow vanishing point: It is actually the end of the vertical line from the LS. It is also the point where the vertical line from the LS hits the ground. Shadows will radiate out from this point.

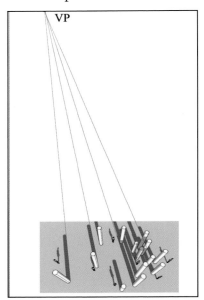

Figure 2-52. *Note that all the shadows share a VP in this figure.*

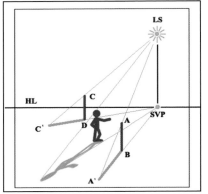
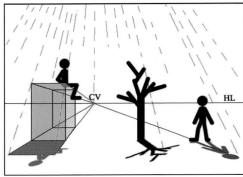

Figures 2-53 and 2-54. *Note that the sun hits the ground creating the SVP (shadow vanishing point.) The length of each shadow is determined by hitting the top of the object, and connecting the line coming from the SVP, via the bottom of each object.*

Figures 2-55. *Though the shadow vanishing point is outside of the picture frame, all the shadows cast by the bike poles share the same vanishing point. Photo by Wenhai Ma*

The following two workshops show how the shadow of a box is obtained. Note the differences: In Workshop I, the light source is behind the box and the shadow vanishing point ends right on the eye level, or the horizon line. I made the box transparent to begin with so I can see the back corner.

Send light convergence lines through all top corners of the object (some may end up inside your object). Then send shadow convergence lines through all the corresponding bottom corners until they intersect with the light lines. This will mark the extreme edges of your shadow.

Note in Workshop I, the light source is behind the box and ends right on the HL, or the eye level. In Workshop II, the light source is next to the box so it is below the eye level, or the HL, as shown in figures below.

Figure 2-56. *Illustration by Wenhai Ma for* Swan's Gift, *text by Brenda Seabrooke, Candlewick Press, 14" x 22", watercolor and India ink on paper, 1995. Note the shadows form the fence. Though they are not perfect straight lines, they go in the same direction, seemingly toward the same vanishing point.*

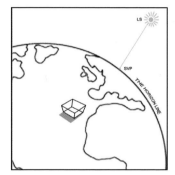 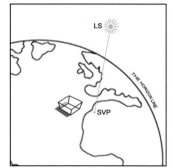

Figures 2-57 and 2-58.

I.   II.

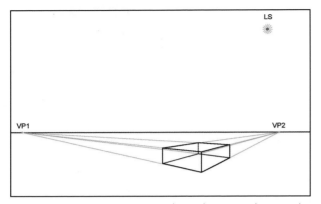

Figure 2-59. *Determine the HL or EL (eye level) and the LS (light source). Place the box on the ground.*

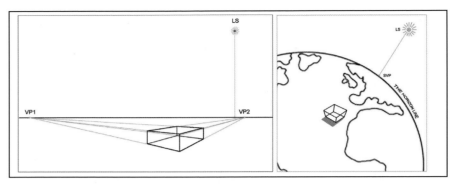

Figure 2-60. *Draw a vertical line from the LS and establish the SVP (shadow vanishing point). In this case, the SVP ends on the eye level (EL or HL) and the light source is behind the object.*

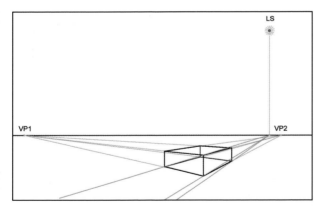

Figure 2-61. *Draw lines from the SVP through the bottom corners of the box.*

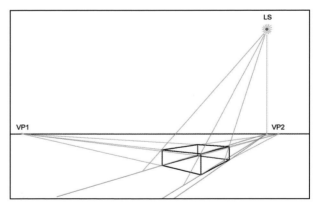

Figure 2-62. *Draw lines from the LS and go through these same three corners, but on the top.*

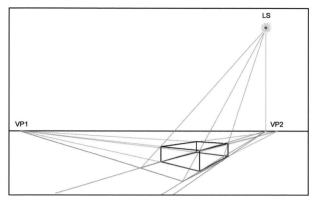

Figure 2-63. *Connect the points where these lines intersect with the shadow convergence lines and form the shadow. Note the shadow is also lined up with the VP on each side.*

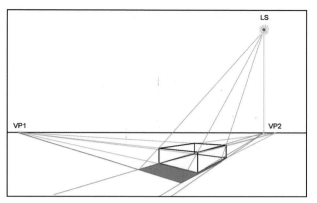

Figure 2-64. *Finished drawing. Photoshop sketches by Wenhai Ma.*

WORKSHOP II

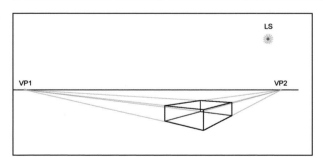

Figure 2-65. *Determine the HL or EL (eye level) and the LS (light source). Place the box on the ground.*

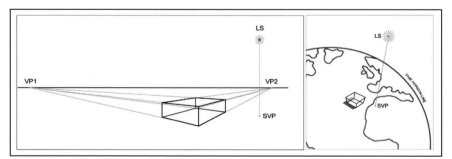

Figure 2-66. *Draw a vertical line from the LS and establish the SVP (shadow Vanishing Point). In this case, the SVP does not end on the eye level (EL or HL) but it goes below it. Also note that the light source is on the side of the object*

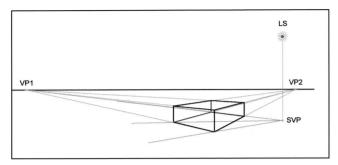

Figure 2-67. *Draw lines from the SVP through the bottom corners of the box.*

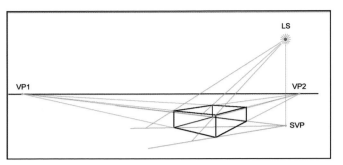

Figure 2-68. *Draw lines from the LS through the top three corners of the box.*

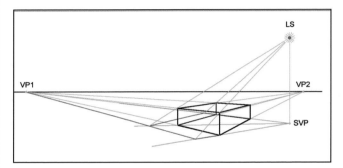

Figure 2-69. *Connect the points where these lines intersect with the shadow convergence lines and form the shadow. Note the shadow is also lined up with the VP on each side.*

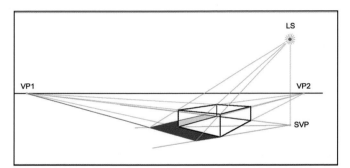

Figure 2-70. *The light gray area of the shadow will not be seen if the box is solid.*

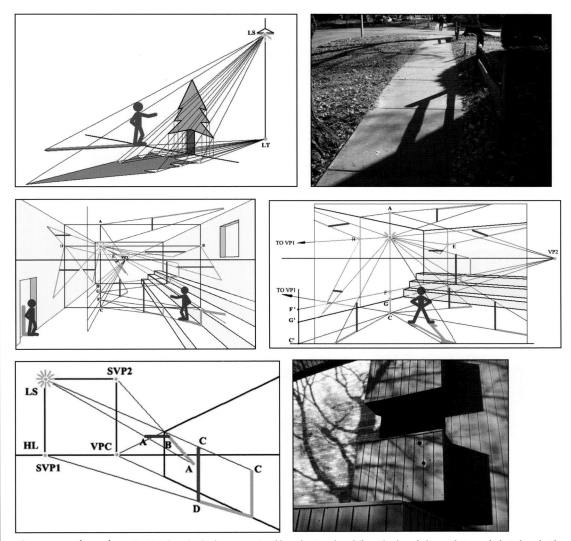

Figures 2-71 through 2-76. *Note how the shadows are cast and how they travel on different levels and planes. Photos and Photoshop sketches by Wenhai Ma.*

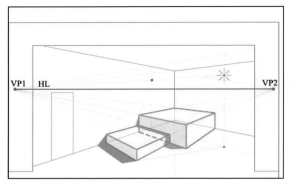

Figures 2-77. *Note how the shadows are cast by the two platforms, with the LS on the right. AutoCAD sketch by Shang Yan Liang.*

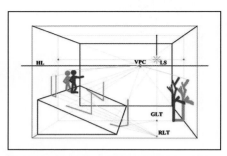

Figures 2-78 and 2-79. *Note that shadows of the poles on the ramp follow the angle and how the shadow of the tree travels from the floor to the wall. AutoCAD sketch by Shang Yan Liang. Photo by Wenhai Ma.*

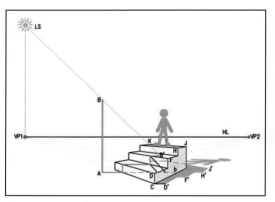

Figures 2-80 and 2-81. *Note how shadows climb up along the steps. AutoCAD sketch by Shang Yan Liang. Photo by Wenhai Ma.*

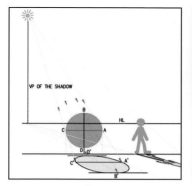

Figures 2-82 and 2-83. *Note how the shadows are cast particularly for the disc. AutoCAD sketch by Shang Yan Liang. Photo by Wenhai Ma.*

Figures 2-84 through 2-86. *Details of illustrations for Swan's* Gift *by Wenhai Ma, text by Brenda Seabrooke, a Candlewick Press book, 1995, watercolor and India ink. These illustrations show shadows cast by moonlight.*

Additional Hints

Light radiates out in all directions. When the light source is directly above an object, then the object will cast shadows in all directions.

Shadows can be cast on a number of surfaces. For example, when an object is sitting on a table, then there will be a different shadow vanishing point for the object (which will be on the tabletop) and for the table (which is on the floor).

When the light source is the sun or the moon, the shadow vanishing point is on the horizon directly below the light source.

Draw Reflections in the Water

Some artists will draw the reflected image as an exact, upside-down version of the direct image. This may be fine for stylized paintings, but realistic painting requires a more accurate representation of what your eyes actually see.

When viewing a scene of reflections in water, you are seeing the actual objects in the scene and their reflected images from two different viewing angles. Of course, the reflected image you see in the water bounces off the surface of the water. Nevertheless, you see the reflected scene from an angle of view as far below the surface of the water as your eyes are above the water.

Overall, reflections of objects will be somewhat darker and dimmer than objects seen directly. Also, the closer the water is to the viewer, the more poorly it reflects an image of the earth and sky. Water directly below the viewer reflects only faint images while distant water reflects almost, but not quite as well as a mirror.

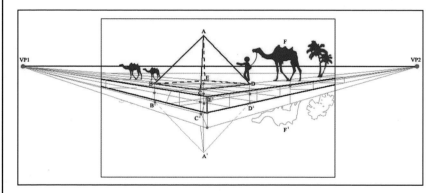

Figure 2-87. *This figure shows how the reflection is obtained. Note the reflected images are not exact, upside-down versions of the direct images. Photoshop sketch by Wenhai Ma.*

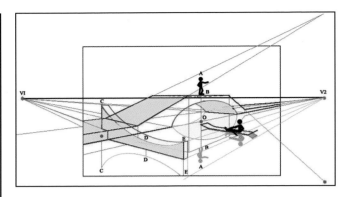

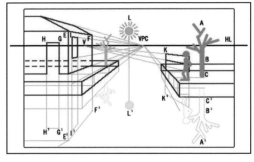

Figures 2-88 to 90. *These figures show how the reflection is obtained. Note the reflected images are not exact, upside-down versions of the direct images. Photoshop sketches by Wenhai Ma.*

Figures 2-91 to 96. *These figures are examples of portraying reflections. All photo and artworks by Wenhai Ma*

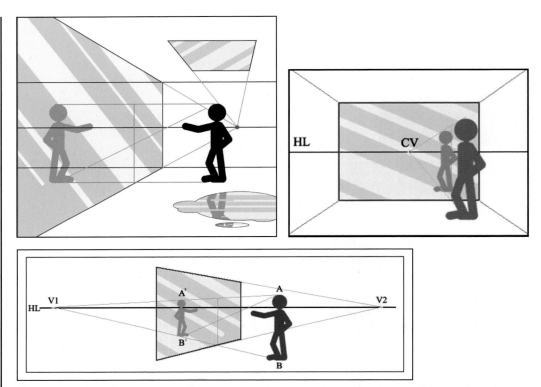

Figures 2-97 through 2-99. *Mirror reflections are very similar to water reflections. These figures may help you understand how to obtain images in mirrors.*

Diffused Perspectives & Tricky Perspective Problems

In oriental artworks, particularly in traditional Chinese and Japanese artworks, many times we see scroll paintings and wood block prints with landscape that does not follow the "perspective method" as it is understood in the western concept. This can be taken as an artistic or theatrical interpretation, or forced perspective. Occasionally I allow myself to adjust my perspective slightly in order to better showcase my design concept.

Figure 2-100. *Copy of a section of scroll painting* A City of Cathay, *Original by Zhang Ze-duan, painted during 1101-1124, Chinese ink and watercolor on silk. Note that in this enormous multi-scene montage, the HL is not shown in this picture and there are many "vanishing points" since it is a panorama or a "collage". It is sized 30' x 1', so it does not follow the one-point or whatever-point perspective method. However, there are still perspective concepts and sense involved – the objects get smaller in scale and faded in color as they go away from the foreground.*

Figure 2-101. A Pleasant Scene *by an anonymous Chinese artist, Yuan Dynasty (1279-1368).*

Figure 2-102. *Section of the Chinese painting* The Night Revels of Han Xizai *by Gu Hongzhong (937–975), Collection of the Palace Museum in Beijing. Chinese painter during the Five Dynasties and Ten Kingdoms period of Chinese history. This remarkable piece is a painted scroll with ink and colors on silk, approximately 131.3' x 11.3', depicting Han Xizai, a minister of Li Yu. Note this narrative panorama painting is split into five distinct sections: Han Xizai listens to the pipe, watches dancers, takes a rest, plays string instruments, and then sees guests off. As with other scrolls, Gu's work is meant to be viewed right-to-left. The perspective however, is meant to move along with the viewer's eyes, instead of the normal fixed point of view..*

Figure 2-103. The Imperial Farming and Weaving Scene, *woodblock print illustration by anonymous artist of the Qing Dynasty, 6" x 6", the collection of the author.*

Figure 2-104. *Reproduction of* Rain at Shinyanagibashi, *by Katsushika Hokusai (1760 – 1849), Japanese master artist and printmaker of the* ukiyo-e *("pictures of the floating world") school. Woodblock print, 8 ¾" x 6", collection of the author. Katsushika Hokusai's work was influence by western art, especially Dutch art. Though the perspective looks good, if we check the piece carefully, the planks on the wooden bridge do not all vanish on the same vanishing point. This also happens in some of his other pieces, and lots of Chinese and Japanese classical artworks.*

Work on a Slanted Roof

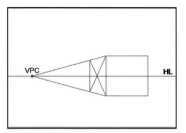

Figure 2-105. *Step 1: draw an "X" on the wall and obtain the center point from the "X".*

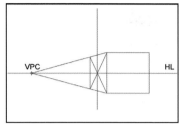

Figure 2-106. *Step 2: Bring it up vertically.*

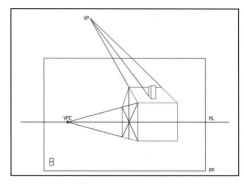

Figure 2-107. *Step 3: Determine the height of the roof by eyeball and figure out the angle of the roof. AutoCAD sketch by Shang Yan Liang.*

The Distance between Light Poles

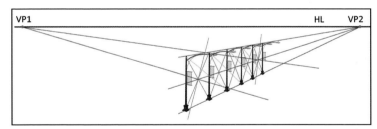

Figure 2-108. *AutoCAD sketch by Shang Yan Liang.*

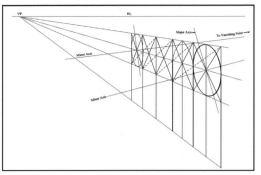

Figures 2-109 and 2-110. The Piazza, Covent Garden *by Thomas and Paul Sandby, watercolour and pen and ink over graphite, around 1765. Reproduction by Wenhai Ma, pencil and Photoshop.*

The Grid Perspective Method

Figure 2-111. *Portrait of Leon Battista Alberti (1404 – 1472), an Italian architect, artist, author, poet and philosopher. Drawing by Wenhai Ma, 2010.*

The stage "Grid Perspective Method" was probably based on Renaissance humanist polymath Alberti's "Grid Perspective Method" or "The Tiled Floor Elevation Method".

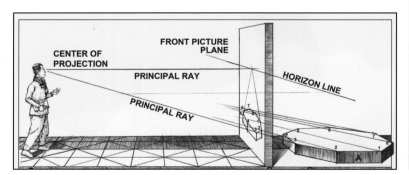

Figures 2-112 and 2-113. *In 1457, Alberti discovered a way of tracing natural perspectives and affecting the diminution of figures, as well as a method of reproducing small objects on a large scale; these were very ingenious and fascinating discoveries, of great value for the purposes of art. These figures show his studies of the objects seen through a piece of glass and a transparent grid that could be placed in front of a scene as an aid to drawing in perspective.*

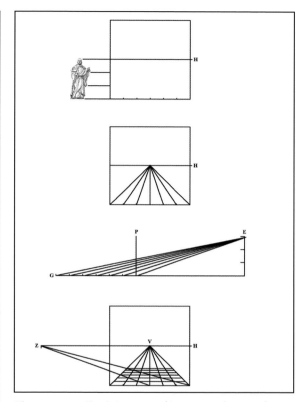

Figure 2-114. *Alberti's Construction* (Costruzione legittima). *1 The base of the picture is divided into* **braccia** *(one third of the height of a man.) The height of the man at the front plane of the picture gives the level of the horizon, H. 2. The* **braccio** *divisions are joined to the perspective focus, V, to give the orthogonals. 3. In side elevation, lines are drawn from* **braccio** *divisions behind the picture plane P to the eye at E. The points of intersection on P are noted. 4. The levels of the points of intersection are marked at the side of the picture plane, and locate the horizontal divisions of the tiles. Z is the 'distance' point, though Alberti only mentions using one diagonal to check the construction. Sketches reproduced by Wenhai Ma.*

The Grid Perspective Method is taught in scene design classes everywhere. Workshop III demonstrates the Grid Perspective Method for Theatre step by step.

It should be helpful to have an understanding of the HL – the horizon line, or the EL – the eye level, before get started, either when you work on a freehand perspective drawing or a grid perspective drawing.

Determine the HL

It is very important to establish the HL before anything else. The observer gets an absolutely unique view depending on where he/she sits and observes.

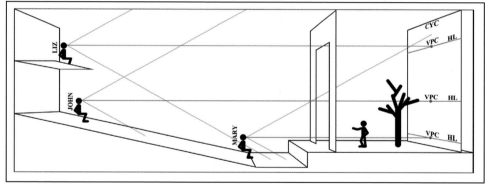

Figure 2-115. *Mary's HL is quite low, so she sees less of the floor. John's HL is close to the mid-way point so he sees the floor well. Liz's HL is really high so she sees lots of the floor. Thus, when you sketch, where to put the HL or where you sit will determine how much of the floor and top of the scenic elements you will see.*

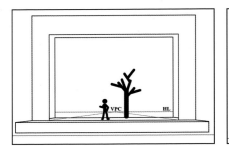
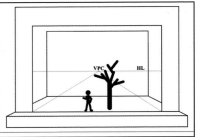
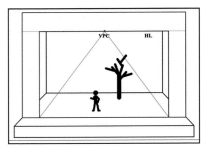

Figures 2-116 through 2-118. *The three figures show the different view points of Mary, John and Liz. Photoshop sketches by Wenhai Ma.*

WORKSHOP III

It is a good idea to tape your drafting paper on the center of the drafting table so you'll have enough room for the lines beyond the pictures – the ground plan and the elevation. Use the parallel and triangles to guide your lines.

Step 1: Here we see a typical "box set" on a proscenium stage. There are four walls on which there are a window, a door and a picture. On the floor, there is a table and a stool. Through the window, we see the cyclorama. There are also four sets of masking – legs and borders. See *Figure 2-119.*

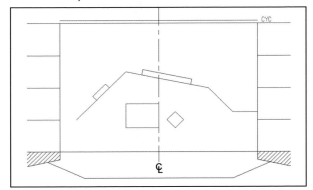

Step 2: Lay grid on the floor – the GP. The stage floor is 36'-0" in width and 24'-0" in depth. Divide the floor into squares — say 3'-0" for each so there are 96 squares on the stage floor. The more squares you have (making each square smaller), the more accurate your perspective will be. However, if

Figure 2-119. *Step 1. The GP (Grid Perspective).*

there are too many squares over your GP, you may find it difficult to read the lines
and therefore, it can become confusing. You may determine the size and number of
squares according to how complicated your design is. I recommend that you work on
a large scale (¼" or ½") if your design is complicated with lots of scenic pieces and
levels. Obviously, this box set design is rather simple. See *Figure 2-120.*

Step 3: Locate the FE below the GP, aligned. Indicate the proscenium opening, say,
36" x 26", according to whatever scale you are using. Find the stage floor and the GP
in perspective.

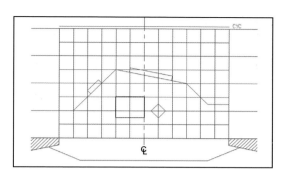

Figure 2-120. *Step 2. The GP.*

Put the HL a little above halfway of the proscenium height. Remember: the higher
the HL is, the more of the stage floor will be seen. It is up to you where to put the HL — just
use your common sense to determine the HL. Imagine yourself sitting somewhere close to
the center line, behind the stage manager's desk for technical rehearsals. You may not want to
imagine the view from the very first row or the last row in the balcony back at the back of the
house. Locate the VPC close to the middle of the HL. Lower the grid distance from the GP
to the FE and mark the distances on the PP, or mark the PP into 12 equal distances, as spaced
on the GP. Connect the marked distances with the VPC and get the 12 equal distances in
perspective view.

You need to keep some space between the GP and the FE so you'll have room to obtain the
MD (Measuring Distance).

Determine the OP (Observation Point). The OP is the point between the observer's eyes. The
VPC (vanishing point center) is the OP on the HL. Sit neither too close to nor too far away
from the stage, so you may get a good angle to see the whole picture and the stage floor. See
Figure 2-121.

Step 4: The plaster line (PL) is the line running from the back on one side of the proscenium
arch to the other proscenium. Take the distance between the plaster line and the OP as the

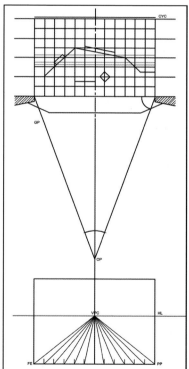

Figure 2-121. *Step 3. The GP and the FE.*

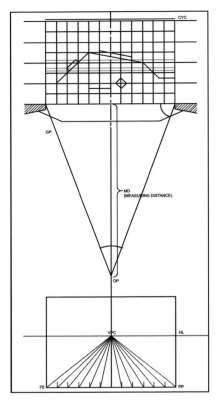

Figure 2-122. *Step 4. The GP and the FE.*

MD (Measuring Distance). Note the OP is aligned with the VPC on the HL on the FE below. The distance between the plaster line and the OP on the GP is called the MD (Measuring Distance). See *Figure 2-122.*

Step 5: Take the MD and put it on the HL on the EF starting from the VPC, on either side, or both sides. Now we've obtained another MP (Measuring Point) on the HL. Obtain the stage depth on the FE: On the GP, the stage floor is 24' -0". So, the end of the 8th square is how deep it goes. Get this depth by counting from the corner of either side of the PP. The end of the 8th square on the PP is actually the depth of the 8th square on the GP. Connect the 9th point with the MP on the HL of the FE with a diagonal line crossing 9 lines on the stage. Then the depth for each square is obtained by drawing a horizontal line right on each of the crossing points. See *Figure 2-123.*

Step 6: Draw horizontal lines on each of the crossing points to obtain the depth of each square. We now see the stage floor with the grid. See *Figure 2-124.*

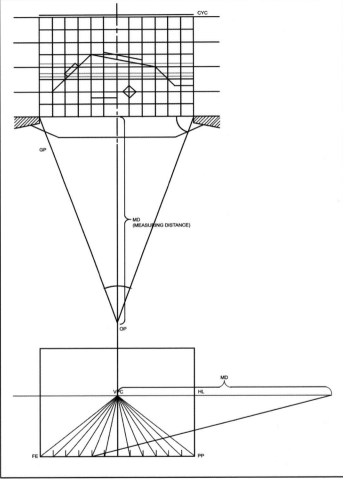

Figure 2-123. *Step 5. The GP and the FE.*

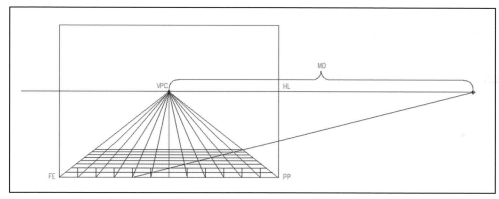

Figure 2-124. *Step 6. The FE.*

Step 7: Transfer the bottom lines of the setting to the floor on the FE by marking all the turning points and connecting them. See *Figure 2-125*.

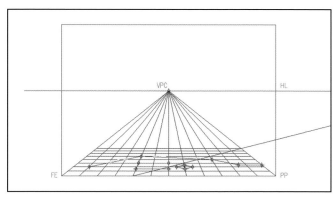

Figure 2-125. *Step 7. The FE.*

Step 8: Bring all the points up vertically. Now the question is how to figure out the height of each vertical line. Let's say all the walls are 9'-10" high, the door is 8'-0", and the window itself is 5'-0" high and 3'-0" from the floor. The picture itself is 2'-6" high, 4'-0" from the floor. The table is 2'-6" high, the stool is 1'-6" high. The borders are trimmed 26'-0" from the stage floor.

Find the true height of each object on the left or right side of plaster line. Let's start with the first vertical line on stage right. Mark the true height of the wall (9'-10") on the corner point of the down stage floor. Then draw a line to the VPC. Let's call it TH-Wall (True Height-Wall). See *Figure 2-126.*

Step 9: Bring the bottom of each point horizontally to the edge of the stage right floor, and then bring it up vertically till it *meets* the line from the TH-Wall to the VPC. Now we see the height of the wall in that particular spot. Then bring the height back to where the wall actually is. See *Figure 2-127.*

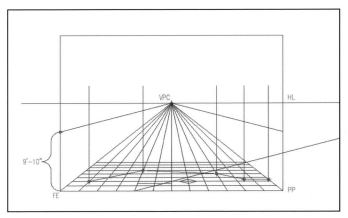

Figure 2-126. *Step 8. The FE.*

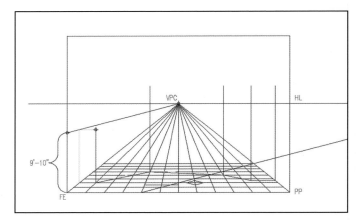

Figure 2-127. *Step 9. The FE.*

Step 10: Obtain the second height, that of the other end of the wall, with the same method. See *Figure 2-128.*

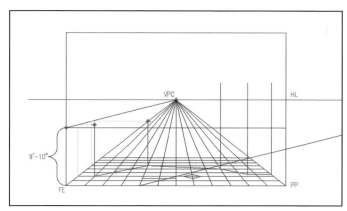

Figure 2-128. *Step 10. The FE.*

Step 11: Obtain the height for all the walls with the same method. See *Figure 2-129.*

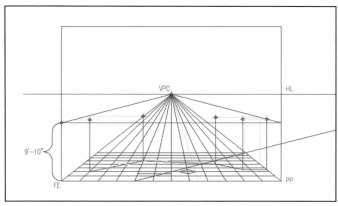

Figure 2-129. *Step 11. The FE.*

Step 12   Connect all the heights and we get all the walls. Obtain the heights of the door and widow with the same method. Mark the TH-Window (5'-0") and TH-Door (7'-0") on the corner point of the down stage floor, same way as for the walls. See *Figure 2-130.*

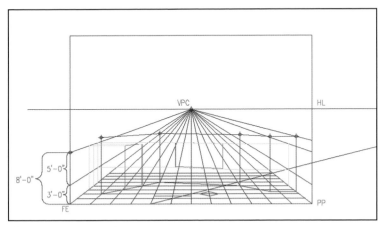

Figure 2-130. *Step 12. The FE.*

Step 13: Do the same for the furniture. See *Figure 2-131.*

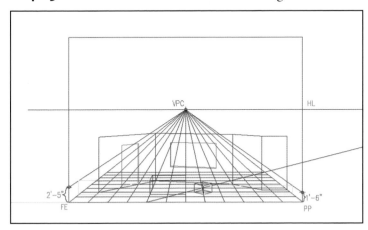

Figure 2-131. *Step 13. The FE.*

Step 14: Do the same for a 6-foot-tall actor. See *Figure 2-132.*

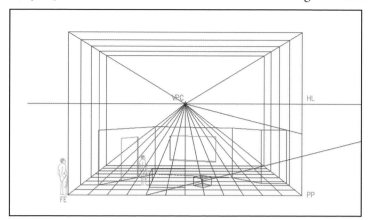

Figure 2-132. *Step 14. The FE.*

Step 15: Clean up the FE. See *Figure 2-133.*

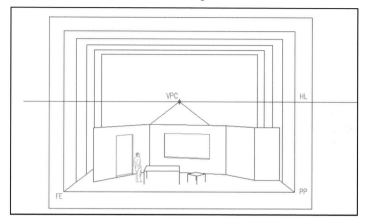

Figure 2-133. *Step 15. The FE.*

Step 16: Freehand work on the details of the room such as the picture, the door, the window, the molding on the walls, the furniture, the rug on the floor, and the scene outside. See *Figure 134.* All AutoCAD sketches by Shang Yan Liang.

You can use this method as your perspective template and then work on the details freehand.

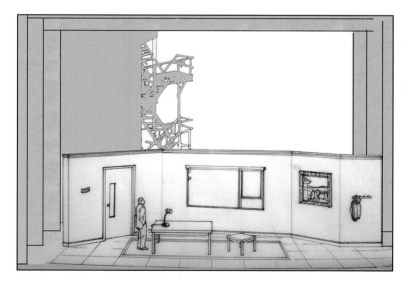

Figure 2-134. *Step 16: Final sketch by Wenhai Ma.*

Use a Stage Photo as a Template

You may also take a photograph of the theatre and use it as a template for perspective and work out the scenic details freehand. The figures below show how a perspective sketch is established by using a black box theatre photograph.

Figure 2-135. *A black box theatre.*

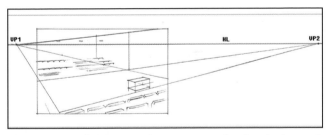 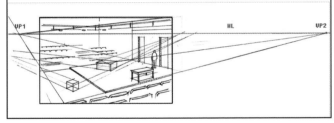

Figure 2-136 and 2-137. *Trace the main perspective lines from the photograph. Find out the HL, the vanishing points of the main elements. Freehand finish the sketch. Sketches by Wenhai Ma.*

Figure Perspective on the Stage

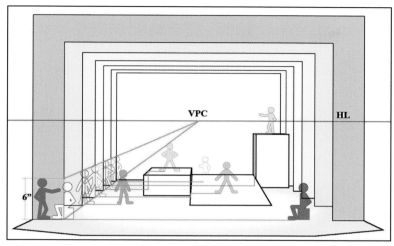

Figure 2-138. *This sketch shows how a six-foot tall actor is seen in different distances and on different levels. Photoshop sketch by Wenhai Ma.*

3

SHADOW & LIGHT

"You should get away from the intoxication of real light and digest your impression in the reduced light in the room. Then you can get drunk on sunshine again."

Pierre-Auguste Renoir (1841–1919)
French artist, leading painter in the development of the Impressionist style.

DRAWING BY WENHAI MA

Unlike the Oriental art and paintings of the Medieval times, shadow and light has been an integral feature in Western art particularly since the Renaissance. In reality, everything around us is three dimensional. In drawing and painting, however, we work on a two dimensional surface. To successfully mimic realism, we must have linear perspective, color perspective, and shadow and light. We can hardly imagine truly three-dimensional appearance in any painting that has no shadow and light.

The Theatrical Light

Mastery of shadow and light is an integral part of drawing. It can be as challenging and tricky to master as color. In most fine art schools, shadow and light studies are an important part of the curriculum. It is an absolutely essential foundation before coloring. It is one of the most important skills in "plastic art." Look at the old master works of Leonardo da Vinci, Rembrandt, William Turner and Picasso. The vivid and vital figures they portrayed do not depend only on colors but also on shadow and light. If we pay attention to the drawing studies they did early in their careers, we will find they all had solid training in drawing, and shadow and light studies. And from their watercolor and oil works, we will find that they all mastered ways to "sculpt" the three-dimensionality on paper and canvas, to deal with shadow and light though each of them established his own remarkable style. Furthermore, in many of their works, we may find the ways they dealt with shadow and light are rather more "theatrical" than "realistic."

Figures 3-1 and 3-2. *Look at Rembrandt's the* Night Watch. *The focused light is amongst the crowd as if it is hit by a spotlight. Furthermore, doesn't it appear that some of the shadow and light was cast by some sort of "candle light" secretly held by the characters? In Rembrandt's self-portrait (copied by Wenhai Ma), we also see the face is beautifully and theatrically lit. Such complex lighting effects are also often used in movies.*

Figure 3-3. *Illustration by Wenhai Ma for* Swan's Gift, *text by Brenda Seabrooke, Candlewick Press, 14" x 22", watercolor and India ink on paper, 1995. Note the theatrical light used to focus the main action.*

Figure 3-4. *Chinese Emperor Qian-Long's portrait in oil painted by Italian Qing imperial court painter Giuseppe Castiglione (1688—1766). The artist combined the Oriental concept with the Western techniques but omitted shadows in this piece. "The Oriental attitude" at that time did not appreciate a portrait with one side of the face darker than the other and a landscape with shadows — the shadow on a person's nose was either thought to be a tragic defect or perhaps some paint spilled by accident.*

Figure 3-5. *Illustration by Wenhai Ma for* Red Means Good Fortune *(Viking, 1994.) Text by Barbara Diamond Goldin. The shadow and light portrayed in this illustration is subtle and soft.*

Figure 3-6. Broadcast, *a musical premiere, University of Nebrsaka-Lincoln, set designed by Wenhai Ma, 2006. On the stage, most of the time there is more than one light source. Though imitating the natural light sources, we tend to dramatize lighting for the needs of the scene. Note the actor on the stage — there are multiple shadows being cast by him. Photo by Wenhai Ma.*

Figure 3-7. Morning by the Pond *by Wenhai Ma. Oil on board, 30cm x 22cm, 1988. Note the bright light brings vitality to the scene.*

The Focal Point

The focal point is what draws and attracts the viewer's eyes. Place the focal point: the main subject of the picture or in fact the actors' action for this specific moment. In the meantime, the other actors in the picture should lead the eye towards this focal point. The lighting should be subtle.

Figure 3-8. *Illustration by Wenhai Ma for* Swan's Gift, *text by Brenda Seabrooke, Candlewick Press, 14" x 22", watercolor and India ink on paper, 1995. The arrangement of shadow and light, the focal point and the emphasis is rather theatrical in this picture.*

The Contour

In fact, such a "contour" in reality does not exist. We tend to simplify the objects we see everyday and simplify the objects on paper with a "contour". Look the ball in *Figure 3-9* and the bust in *Figure 3-10*. We see the three dimensionality of the ball and the bust because of the contrast between the objects and the background and the shadow and light. The "contours" actually do not exist.

Lines have varied "line weights," or rhythm. The "line weight," or contrast between the objects and the background, can be strong and sharp, or can be weak and subtle. In *Figure 3-11*, the lines are imaginary and simplified. Or, you could say, it is a "simplified vision of three-dimensionality."

Figures 3-9 and 3-10. *Photoshop sketch and photo by Wenhai Ma.*

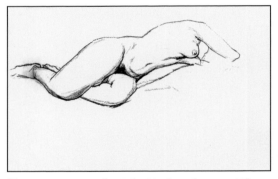

Figure 3-11. *Drawing by Wenhai Ma, charcoal on paper, 20"x 15", 2004.*

Figure 3-12. Dragon, *Chinese calligraphy by Wenbo Ma, Chinese ink on rice paper, 16" x 22", 1986. In Chinese calligraphy, especially in this cursive style, rhythm energy is as much appreciated as the writing. This is a fine example showing the energy and various line weights for the two brushstrokes the artist applied. The calligraphy shows the abstractive movement of the 'dragon,' for this particular character is actually pictographic.*

Values, "Colors of Black"

It is very important for us to learn to deal with black and white well. The color black, depending on the degree or density, can be controlled in different levels of intensity, or grey values. It is very helpful if you have such a sketch in black and white prepared before coloring. In Chinese ink painting art, it is said that *the black ink can be used as five colors.* This is very similar to the value chart we usually see in drawing books.

A stage picture, including the setting and the actors, is actually very similar to a landscape composed with three major values: white (light), black (dark), and grey (mid-tone). The brightness is composed of three major parts: sky (background), ground (floor) and objects (scenery). It is very important to have the relationship built up well between each of the three. Therefore, it is helpful to work out a thumbnail sketch of your rendering's black and white arrangement.

Check how much of each value your sketch has got. For a strong composition, you want the different tonal values to be used in quite different, not similar, amounts. Try this rule to start: "two thirds, one third, and a little bit." For example, two thirds dark in tone, one third light in tone, and a small area or object that's mid-tone.

Check how each of the three major parts are valued and how they are related. Usually, the actors and their surroundingss (objects) are the white (light), the stage floor and the cyclorama (background) is the grey (mid-tone) and the masking is the black (dark), as part of the whole value contrast, or composition. See *Figures 3-14, 3-15*

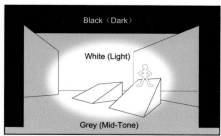

Figure 3-13. *Photoshop sketch by Wenhai Ma.*

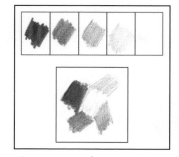

Figures 3-14 and 3-15. *The chart on the left shows the five values created by using an HB pencil. The chart on the right shows the seven hues from Prussian Blue. Sketches by Wenhai Ma.*

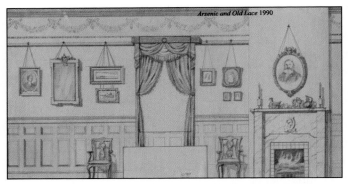

Arsenic and Old Lace 1990

Figure 3-16. *This sketch was created by using a couple of drawing pencils. Paint elevation for* Arsenic and Old Lace *by Wenhai Ma, 15 ½" x 6", 1989.*

Figure 3-17. *Drawing by Wenhai Ma, pencil on paper, 32" x 24", approximately, 1980.*

Figure 3-18. *Drawing by Yaoyao Ma Van As, pencil on paper, 2007.*

Figure 3-19. Apples *by Yaoyao Ma Van As, pencil on paper, 2007.*

Figure 3-20. *This illustration demonstrating dry brush techniques shows the "colors", or values created by black ink. Note the contrast amongst black, white and grey tones. The bill post box is pushed away from the foreground man by high contrast and certain details have been deliberately neglected. Copied by Wenhai Ma, 1972.*

Figure 3-21. *This pencil sketch was made for* A Midsummer Night's Dream *as a shadow and light study before coloring, 3" x 4", pencil on photocopy paper. Sketch by Wenhai Ma.*

Shadows

Shadows are cast by objects – on stage, by actors, scenery and props. Shadows visually help the viewers understand the "objects" are physically grounded. *Figure 3-23* shows the figures are grounded, by the shadow they cast.

Figure 3-22. *Pencil drawing by Wenhai Ma. The shadow cast by the tree roots starts strong and as it moves away from the object, becomes weaker and blurry.*

Figure 3-23. *Illustration for* Red Means Good Fortune *by Wenhai Ma, text by Barbara D. Goldin, Viking, 1995. This illustration shows the lighting effect and atmosphere that can be achieved by using only black watercolor. Watercolor over pencil sketch on watercolor paper, 12" x 11".*

4

PREPARING THE SKETCH

"I saw the angel in the marble and carved until I set him free."

Michelangelo di Lodovico Buonarroti Simon (1475–1564)
Italian Renaissance painter, sculptor, architect, poet, and engineer.

Unless your design is rather simple and you are confident to put the lines on watercolor paper directly, I highly recommend you work on a piece of drafting paper first – to figure out all the major perspective lines. If you work with pencil on your watercolor paper for too long, your paper may become dirty, sketchy, unfriendly to water colors, and even damaged. For the best watercolor effect, the watercolor paper should be kept clean and fresh. As said by J.M.W. Turner: "First of all, respect your paper!"

Figure Out the Perspective

The sketch should be correct in perspective, serving as a draft with most of the details on it – The set within a proscenium arch, the scenic pieces, furniture, props, the backdrop or cyclorama, masking and an actor or more. This sketch can be printed on drafting paper or vellum so it can be traced onto watercolor paper easily. You may work on whatever size is convenient and enlarge or reduce the size as needed.

Workshop I

Step 1

Figure 4-1. *Start with the Stage. Portray your stage proscenium proportionally. If your proscenium arch opening is 36" x 26", then the proportion of your sketch should be proportioned around 1.38 x 1. Note I always include an actor to start with in order to get a sense of proportion.*

Step 2

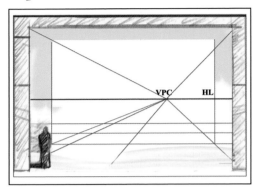

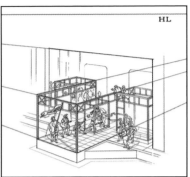

Figure 4-2. *Determine the HL and the VPC. The height of the HL is determined by the viewer – the renderer. If you have a well-treated stage floor with lot of scenic elements, you may like to make the HL higher. When I work on a landscape, I tend to put my HL somewhere below the horizontal middle line of the picture, but for my scene renderings I usually make it higher because I like to show the floor treatment and the scenic elements on the floor. In this sketch, I put the HL a little bit above the half-way point of the picture. I tend not to put my HL right on the horizontal middle line because I don't want to divide my picture equally into half and half. However, when you work on a box set, you may not like to put your HL too close to the top lines of the wall unit. Otherwise the wall units will not show well but rather on the same line as the top. As stated earlier, the VPC is actually the observer's "point of view" – the mid-point between your eyes. I usually put my VPC around the middle of the HL.*

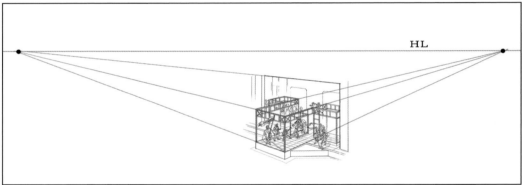

Figures 4-3 through 4-5. *Note that in this rendering for* The Taming of the Shrew, *in order to show my design, I clearly made my HL rather high and my VPC not quite on the center of the HL. I imagined myself sitting in house right. Before this sketch, I tried to present my set from a couple of different angles but eventually I found this was the best angle of all. It is not from an audience's point of view but it shows my design well.*

Step 4

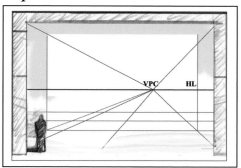

Figure 4-6. *Figure out the major scenic elements on the floor as if you are working on a sketch with the "Grid Perspective Method", you need to figure out the major scenic elements on the stage floor by free hand. Use a ruler to guide the lines if needed. You may also need to figure out the masking legs and borders. Pencil sketches by Wenhai Ma for* **Hamlet**, *20" x 16", Duke University, 1989.*

Step 5

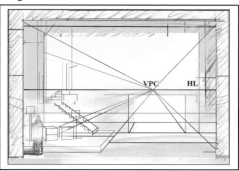

Figure 4-7. *You can eyeball the height of each scenic element. Use a ruler as a guide if needed. Again, remember that all the scenic elements vanish on the same HL except for raked platforms.*

Step 6

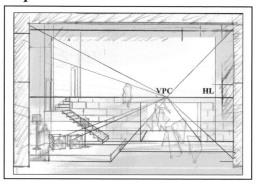

Figure 4-8. *Place furniture and other scenic elements. Remember to use the "boxes" to help figure out the perspective.*

Step 7

Figure 4-9. *Place Actor(s) in the set. It is absolutely necessary to put at least one actor in the sketch so we may tell the proportions and their relationship to the sets just as we do for models. However, be careful not to let your actors cover too much of the setting. The purpose for a scene rendering is to present the design. It is not a book illustration.*

Figure 4-10. Because the set was quite simple, I included quite a few actors as part of the setting.

Figure 4-11. Trace the sketch down on watercolor paper on a light table. Trim the watercolor paper to the desired size. Tape your sketch on the back of the watercolor paper. I usually use a sharpened H pencil because it makes it easy to portray the details, especially the perspective lines. Another advantage is that the H pencil lines will stay visible after coloring. Make the lines lightweight because the traced lines need to be polished and reinforced anyway. As for watercolor paper, high-quality is always a preference. I usually use cold press, as it is good for the wet-into-wet effect. It would be good to have a light table for tracing, though occasionally you may do it on the window!

Because the traced lines are clumsy, mechanical and lack vitality, you will need to take your time to work on the lines. Again, a sharpened H pencil is a good option for working on the perspective, and finalizing the lines. Because it is very easy to smudge your sketch with your hands when sketching at this stage, preparing a piece of tracing paper with a cutout in it and using it as a protective cover may be a good idea. Work on the small area through the cutout. You may even have this protective cover taped down if you need to work on a specific area for a while. You will still need a ruler to reinforce your straight lines unless the intended effect is that of a sketchy free hand drawing.

Step 9

Figure 4-12. *Tape the sketch on the back of the watercolor paper. I usually work on the rough side because of the texture.*

Step 10

Figure 4-13. *You may color directly on the "polished" pencil sketch on watercolor paper. However, I usually take an additional step: to ink the lines with India ink, or waterproof ink. I usually use sepia. Black or blue would also work very well. You may use a graphic pen and a fine point fountain pen (ink refillable) for this stage. For a dip graphic pen, you will need bottled ink. I highly recommend you test your waterproof ink before reaching the watercolor paper. It might bleed and not be completely waterproof. Use a scrap of paper, the same as the actual paper you are using, to put on some ink lines. When the ink lines are dry, add a couple of watercolor wash strokes and see if the ink line will bleed and how it reacts to the watercolor.*

I usually use a bit more pressure or weight for the lines than usual – soft pencil lines might get colored and washed away by brush strokes.

Step 11

I usually keep two ink bottles with one containing the original sepia ink and the other contending diluted sepia ink. On the lids, one is marked with letter "D" for "dark", the other "L" for "light". You can simply drop a small amount of ink in the bottle and add some tap water to it. So, when you ink your sketch, you'll have the same ink in two hues – the dark ink is used for strong lines, elements in the foreground, parts that need to be reinforced and strengthened, such as the actors, furniture and platforms and objects in shadow. The light ink is used for elements that are distant from these elements or things in the background such as trees beyond a box set, through the windows, design on the backdrop or on the CYC, actors with minor actions up stage and objects under strong light.

I sometimes even tend to leave lines un-inked for elements that should be pushed far away and portrayed in a very relaxed and subtle manner to have more dimension and depth on the sketch. To understand this better, take a closer look at Rembrandt's etchings. You will find the elements in the foreground are much stronger because the engraved plate was in the acid and etched a lot longer while the elements in the background are lighter because they were in the acid and etched for less time.

Scratching an Accidental Spot

You also need to control the quantity of ink in the nib of the pen to avoid dropping ink on your paper accidentally. Try to keep as little ink in it as possible in the beginning. In case you drop an ink spot on your paper, just wait till it dries and use an X-Acto blade to scratch it away if it is small enough. This will take some practice. You may need to bend the paper a bit so the ink spot is shown as the "spine top". Then work carefully scratching the ink spot, in one direction. This can be done only on high-quality watercolor paper. However, be careful not to scratch too much or the paper can become damaged. You really cannot rely on this method, for the paper may not take paint well enough, depending on the location of such a spot. If, however, you drop a large ink spot and removing it will mess up the paper to the point where it is really noticeable, it is sometimes better to admit defeat and start over on a fresh piece.

Scratching the paper surface is a great way to achieve a rain drop effect though some practice is needed!

You may also use a wet Q-tip, or a cotton ball to rub on the spot gently. Then use a clean wet brush to wash it. After that use a clean paper towel to lift the water. You cannot rely on this technique to remove large spots or areas. If you find you are unsatisfied with most of what you have done, it might be a better idea to re-do the rendering or sketch. You will have a fresh mind to plan the process and a fresh surface to work with.

Figure 4-14. *Note that for this sketch, I used "waterproof ink" but it was not really waterproof – I did not test it - for my lines. The ink bled. Fortunately, I liked it — it was a "happy accident". Illustration by Wenhai Ma, watercolor and ink on paper.*

Figure 4-15. *Scratching an accidental ink spot.*

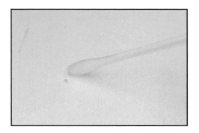

Figure 4-16. *Using a Q-tip cotton ball to erase an accidental spot.*

Figure 4-17. *Illustration for* Swan's Gift *by Wenhai Ma, text by Brenda Seabrooke, a Candlewick Press book, 1995. This illustration shows the different density of the sepia ink used in order to create depth and layers. Watercolor and India ink, 18.5" x 12.5".*

Step 12

Clean up the sketch. Use an eraser to take care of some of the messy pencil lines. However, I usually like to keep some of them because they sometimes add more dimension and depth. It can also add a vivid and dynamic energetic quality to the art.

Figure 4-18. *A finished pencil and ink sketch on watercolor paper.*

Step 13

Save a copy of the original. It is a very good idea to have your well-prepared ink-line sketch photocopied so you'll always have a clean copy for later, should the need arise. For less experienced designers, this step may save time and avoid frustration if the coloring does not turn out well. You may find it easier to have the whole thing traced to watercolor paper with this clean copy, rather than spending hours re-sketching from scrap.

It is sometimes also a good idea to have this sketch scanned so you'll have a digital copy of it and you can try to color it with Photoshop to test the color scheme, even the lighting effect.

If possible, you may even like to have your sketch printed on light weight watercolor paper. Thus, you may test colors and explore techniques on the copies. In this case, you need to make sure to have your watercolor paper trimmed to the same size as the standard paper sizes for your laser printer: 8 ½" x 11", or 11" x 17". Watercolor paper weights 140 lb or 90 lb should work well. However, you might encounter the odd paper jam!

I sometimes have my pencil/ink sketches scanned, adjust the contrast and brightness to my liking, and then print them out onto light-weight but high-quality watercolor paper from a laser printer. I sometimes even color directly on the printed pencil/ink sketches. It saves me a step though I sometimes like to reinforce some of the lines by using a sharp pencil and a pen with India ink.

Shadow & Light Study Sketch

It is quite helpful if you figure out the lighting and atmospheric effect by sketching on a small photocopy of your sketch. This step can be done with a pencil or Photoshop.

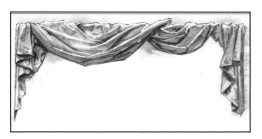

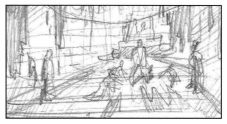

Figure 4-23. *Thumbnail by Wenhai Ma for* Macbeth. *Pencil on paper, 3 ½" x 2 ¼". Note this thumbnail is rather small and rough. It served only as a "reminder" of the shadow and light arrangement I planned before rendering.*

Figures 4-19 through 4-22. *Shadow and light study sketches by Wenhai Ma for various rendering projects. HB, 2B pencils on photocopies of pencil sketches. Sized around 11" x 8 ½", 2009-10.*

Pencil Sketching Techniques

Blocking

Figure 4-24. *Use a piece of paper to cover the edge you want to protect. Apply the strokes from the protective paper towards your sketch. Remove the protective paper and you'll see a clean edge cut from the pencil strokes. Colored pencils used: Dark Blue & Dark Brown.*

Stenciling

Figures 4-25 and 4-26. *Use two pieces of paper and masking tape to cover the areas you want to protect. Apply strokes from either direction carefully. Remove the protective paper and you'll see the sketched area with a clean edge cut on each side. Colored pencils used: Dark Blue & Dark Brown.*

Blocking and Erasing

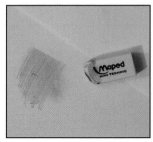

Figure 4-27. *Apply pencil strokes on your sketch. Use a piece of paper to cover the areas you want to protect. Erase the part you do not want to keep, from the protective paper towards your sketch. Remove the protective paper and you'll see a clean edge cut from the pencil strokes. Pencil used: HB.*

Smudging with Tissue

Figure 4-28. *Apply pencil strokes on your sketch. Use a piece of tissue to smudge certain areas and make them appear soft. To achieve this effect, a soft pencil in the "B" category – HB or 2B, is preferred.*

Erasing out a White Spot

Figures 4-29 and 4-30. *Cut a hole in the desired shape and size on a piece of tracing paper. Place it over your pencil shaded area. Position the cut hole right on the desired spot. Use an eraser to go over the area carefully. Remove the tracing paper and you'll see a nice clean white spot. Such techniques can be used for obtaining white lines, stars, etc.*

Color Scheme Study Sketch

Now that you have copies of your original as back ups, you should be fearless to explore the lighting effect and color scheme, and try some techniques on them.

Figures 4-31 and 4-32. *Color studies with Photoshop on scanned sketches. Note that by doing this, I obtained a clear vision of my color scheme, the lighting effect and even brush strokes I may apply later.*

Figure 4-33. *A color study sketch for* He Who Gets Slapped, *watercolor over pencil sketch on photocopy paper, 5 ½''''x 4'', 1993.*

Mood and Atmosphere

"Without atmosphere a painting is nothing."

Rembrandt H. van Rijn (1606–1669)
Dutch painter and etcher.

Atmosphere is the mood that the designer is trying to put into a rendering.
Learn to control light and depth as you build atmospheric renderings. Gradually build block of color, adjusting lighting conditions to suit the desired mood.

One of the most important aims in theatre design rendering is to capture a sense of a theatrical scene, with mood and atmosphere, and this is a quality that should be conveyed in a personal way, without being over-anxious about depicting exactly what is there. As theatre designers, we are "telling a story, not picture-taking".

The greatest enemy of a rendering is deadness — dull, flat color, without any lighting effect and mood and atmosphere. On the stage, visually most of these aspects are created by lighting and smoke. Tone is definitely a weapon.

When you work on a rendering, understand the kind of performance is a great help. Is it a Drama? Opera? Ballet? Dance? Classical? Modern? Tragedy? Comedy? Musical? Fairy tale? Farce? is it light or dark? warm or cool? Is it lyrical or musical? What is it going to say in this particular scene or moment? Each of these will certainly have a different approach expressing a unique mood and atmosphere.

The experiences can be observed and studied from paintings and from the theatre. The mood and atmosphere can be exercised and planned around the shadow and light study sketches and the color scheme study sketches. See *Figures 4-34 through 4-40* and note how the mood and atmosphere is portrayed in each piece. The watercolor wet-in-wet technique is an efficient method for such an effect.

Figures 4-34 through 4-37. *Illustrations by Wenhai Ma, for various articles and books. Watercolor, pencil or India ink on paper.*

Figure 4-38. *Rendering by Wenhai Ma for* Three Sisters, *watercolor, India ink on paper, 16" x 9 ½", 1993.*

Figures 4-39 and 4-40. *Renderings by Wenhai Ma for* Hamlet *by Shakespeare, Duke University, 1998, watercolor, India ink and pencil. 20" x 13".*

Stretching the Paper

Because wet paint causes the fiber in watercolor paper to swell and it can make the paper buckle or warp the surface, it is a very good idea to have the paper properly stretched before starting to work so the paper stays flat when using large quantities of water. This can take some extra time but it is worth it. This is beneficial for paper in all different weights, as once the paper is stretched you are free to use as much water as needed. Stretching works by soaking the paper to expand the fibers, and then taping it flat to dry.

There are a couple of ways to stretch the paper, depending on the size, the duration of time you will work on it and with the wet-into-wet techniques you intend to apply.

The most common way is to use gummed tape.

Stretching the paper with gummed tape.

You will need:

- Gummed brown-paper tape, 2" wide
- A clean wooden drawing board
- A plastic tray about 4" deep, large enough for the whole paper to be dipped in
- A clean foam sponge
- A pair of scissors
- A #6 flat brush

Figure 4-41. *Tools needed for stretching the paper.*

Step 1

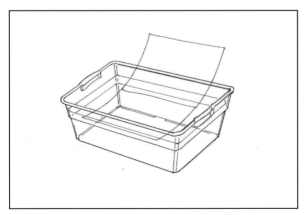

Figure 4-42. *Immersing the paper. You can either dip the whole paper in a tray with water, or just use a large soft flat brush to wet it.*

Step 2

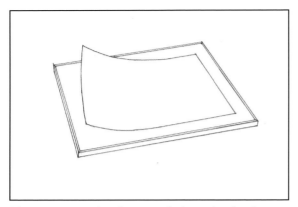

Figure 4-43. *Smoothing the paper on the drawing board. Make sure to have your sketch placed and taped parallel to the edges of the drawing board, for you may want to use your T-square to re-check certain lines.*

Step 3
Smoothing the paper on the drawing board.

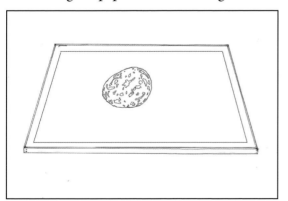

Figure 4-44. *Removing excess water by using the large soft flat brush or a clean sponge.*

Step 4

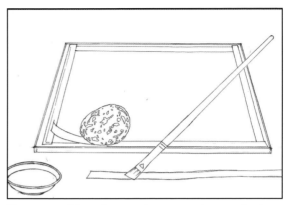

Figure 4-45. *Wetting the gummed tape strips with water and sticking them around the edges of the paper. Press them well and flat.*

For small-sized renderings, you may use regular masking tape to tape around the edges without having the paper soaked in water first. Simply lay the line sketch on the drawing board. Apply 2" masking tape around the border of the sketch. Press the tape well until it is securely attached to the paper and the board. Your rendering will have a nice clean edge when you finish and peel the tape off. Sometimes, you might prefer to have a loose and soft bleed around the rendering and in this case, make the paper a couple of inches larger on each side so you may tape your paper away from the actual rendered area. You will find it easy to work on a well stretched and flat surface. To have your watercolor sketch taped on a drawing board will allow you to adjust the angle and position when you color. Occasionally you can let your watery wash flow for certain effect. To have the sketch taped on the drawing board will also allow you turn your sketch easily as you will find you often have to do.

I occasionally use the old-fashioned way to stretch the paper, mainly for large pieces and for renderings that I may expect will take longer to complete. This is similar to the gummed tape method. Instead of using gummed tape strips, I use regular drawing paper but apply white glue on one side of the paper strips and use them as "gummed" strips. This may work the best in order to keep the paper flat and tight. The disadvantage of this method is that when the rendering is finished, you need to trim it down with an X-acto knife and the remaining paper strips are hard to remove.

In addition to the items needed for stretching the paper with gummed tape, you will need:
- 2"-wide drawing paper strips, 4" longer than the width and height of the rendering.
- White glue in a tray with an opening bigger than the width of a #6 flat brush.

Figure 4-46. *The ink sketch on watercolor paper has been properly taped on the drawing board, ready for coloring.*

5

Pigments & Media

"I found I could say things with colors that I couldn't say in any other way - things that I had no words for."

Georgia Totto O'Keefe (1887–1986)
American artist.

The most common and popular pigments and media we use for scene design renderings are watercolor, acrylic and gouache. Other media such as water-soluble pencils, colored pencils, markers, pastels and oil can also work well. I prefer watercolor over the others. I find watercolor is very handy and effective for creating an atmospheric quality. I also find acrylic and gouache are very good media for paint elevations.

Watercolor

Watercolor has been known since at least ancient Egyptian times. Artists illuminating papyrus scrolls in Egypt, silk and rice paper scrolls in the Orient, manuscripts in the Dark and Middle Ages, all worked with a water medium, usually of an opaque kind. During the European Renaissance times, watercolor techniques were further developed. German artist Albrecht Dürer (1471–1528) is considered among the earliest watercolorists. Later, Baroque artists such as Antony Van Dyck, Claude Lorrain, and Giovanni Benedetto Castiglione made many beautiful watercolors.

Present-day aquarelle, often called transparent watercolor, did not evolve from these forms of painting, though. Aquarelle is the direct descendant of the pen-and-ink-wash drawings made by artists of the Renaissance and Baroque. English artist Paul Sandby (1725 – 1797 or 1809) is called the "Father of Western Watercolor." See *Figure 5-1.*

The most advantageous feature of watercolor is that it is good for representing the theatrical atmosphere, which is what is usually desired by scene designers. I particularly like its subtle nature. Watercolor is also a very popular medium for costume designers in coloring their renderings. In addition, watercolor is very handy for quick color sketches.

Many of the greatest painters in the 19th and early 20th centuries began using watercolor as a major medium. Some were fond of using watercolor to do their color studies before going to the easel with oil. In the past water coloring was required training before painting with oil at art institutions. There's a lot we can learn by studying the methods, palettes, color schemes and techniques of the old masters.

Figure 5-1. Chepstow Castle *Paul Sandby; watercolor with gouache, private collection, Photo ©Agnew's, London, UK.*

Among these are J.M.W. Turner (1775 – 1851), John Singer Sargent (1856-1925), James A McNeill Whistler (1834-1903), Winslow Homer (1836-1910), Edward Hopper (1882-1967), Andrew Wyeth (b. 1917) and more. They developed techniques and made watercolor a medium with tremendous diversity of style.

Acrylic

Acrylic is also a very useful pigment. The colors are bright and sharp, and it has the flexibility of watercolor while also allowing the artist to achieve the same kind of effects as gouache or oil paint. You can water it down without white paint for a somewhat subtle watercolor effect, or you add white to get lighter hues – the opaque colors. You may also use a palette knife to "paint" or "sculpt". It dries with a semi-gloss finish.

The challenge is that it dries fast and the dried paint cannot be reused. Thus, you need to budget your time well. You will also need to get your palette cleaned up each time after use, for the dried paint will become hard and difficult to remove.

Gouache

Gouache (pronounced as "gwash") has been used since the times before the Renaissance. In the 18th century, Paul Sandby first used the painting technique extensively, and later the Pre-Raphaelites. Opaque techniques were further popularized by the Impressionists and Post-Impressionists. Poster colors or gouache became available after the First World War.

Gouache is a water-based opaque pigment. It usually contains gum arabic and some honey. Unlike watercolor, white is often used in gouache, as in acrylics and oils. The paint is applied without much water, and you have to mix a color with white if you want to make it lighter. It isn't used as a stain like most watercolor pigment. It is widely used by commercial designers and artists for their works such as graphic, poster, product and industrial designs, illustrations, comics, and theatre designs.

Figure 5-2. *Daisies by Wenhai Ma, watercolor on illustration board, 22" x 19 ½", 1987. Note in this piece, white was not used at all. Instead the white petals of the flowers were obtained by showing the white illustration board itself.*

Figure 5-3. *Rendering by Wenhai Ma for* Medea, *acrylic on watercolor paper, 10" x 7". Note that white was used for all lighter hues.*

In theatre, it is also an ideal pigment for painter's elevations and model coloring. It has a similar feel to oil paint and the colors can be brilliant, flat, vivid and sharp, grey and opaque. Before I went to Carnegie Mellon for my MFA studies, I used gouache for my scene design renderings all the time. This was partly because of the Russian influence at the Central Academy of Drama in Beijing where I studied as a BFA student. I do not use gouache for my renderings nowadays but I still use it for coloring my models and paint elevations. I still enjoy looking at renderings done with gouache by the old master designers and my friends.

Most 20th-century animators used gouache as the primary medium to create an opaque color on a cell, while watercolor was used for backgrounds. Gouache as "poster paint" is desirable for its speed and durability.

Here is a list some of the old and modern masters who enjoyed working with gouache and produced great artworks: Albrecht Dürer (1471-1528) ; Nicholas Hillard (1547-1619); Peter Paul Rubens (1577-1640); Sir Anthony Van Dyck (1599-1641); Nicolas Poussin (1594-1665); Edgar Degas (1834-1917); Egon Schiele (1890-1918); Bridget Riley (1931). Check out their art works and see how they mastered gouache!

Colored Pencils

Colored pencils are probably the most "fear free" medium of all. You may hatch, blend colors and erase as you work with drawing pencils.

The challenge is that you need to have good control of your color scheme and hatch your colored strokes well. You will also need to control your line weight well to get the proper values. Colored pencils are by no means "elementary" because they also require a foundation and grasp of traditional medium skills to make a nice color sketch. You may like to use colored pencils over ink line sketches.

Figure 5-4. *Rendering by Wenhai Ma for* The Storm *by Aleksandr Ostrovsky, gouache on watercolor paper, 8 ½" x 11", 1980. Note that white was used for all lighter hues though it is a bit more opaque than* Figure 5-3, *done with acrylic.*

Water-Soluble Pencils

Figure 5-5. *Water-soluble pencils or watercolor pencils are a versatile cross-over between drawing and painting.*

The water-soluble pencils I usually use are the Lyra Aqua Color set, manufactured in Germany, and the Caran d'Ache Neocolor II set, manufactured in Switzerland. They're soft and glide smoothly across a surface, so it's easy to get a lot of color down. The colors are intense and easily convert into paint when you add water. The only downside is that it's hard to draw a fine line with them; rather pick up some color with a brush instead.

I love them and use them very often for story board thumbnail sketches. They are extremely handy. This medium has the strength of both watercolor and colored pencils. It can be quite charming and beautiful when there are strokes left under the brush wash effect.

The challenge is that it also requires some grasp of watercolor skills and a good comprehension of shadow and light.

Figure 5-6. *Storyboard thumbnail by Wenhai Ma for* The Greeks *, directed by Mel Shapiro, Carnegie Mellon. Water-soluble pencils over blue ball point pen sketch, 5" x 3 ¼", 1983.*

Colored Ink

I use colored ink mostly for my costume renderings and occasionally for my scene renderings. I find them unique and interesting.

Figure 5-7. *A set of inks in various colors.*

I use them with dip pens and enjoy the effects which are unique to this medium. You may use a set of bottled liquid ink, and prepare some empty bottles for mixing additional colors and colors in different tints, or water the ink down to get lighter colors.

The challenge is that you need to control lines well. It also involves careful planning in terms of hatching and laying out the strokes. You also need to be careful not to drop ink on your paper accidentally!

Figure 5-8. *Rendering by Wenhai Ma for the* Tartuffe *by Moliere, colored ink on watercolor paper, 37.5cm x 20.5cm, 1983.*

A nice alternative is to try using watercolors as ink. You can use a watercolor brush to mix the desired color and drop it into the pocket of the pen nib, and draw as if using regular colored ink.

However, if the bottled ink is not waterproof or if you use watercolor as ink, you cannot color on top of the lines. You may use acrylic as "waterproof" colored ink and color on top of the lines. Make sure to clean your pen nib every once in a while, since the acrylic paint dries fast and it may clog up your pen easily.

Markers

Markers are also a very handy medium. They are very popular for industrial design sketches, interior design and architectural design. You might find a set of markers that comes with most of the colors you need. There are also "blenders" for color-mixing. It may be considered a "fearless" medium because it does not require you to really mix or blend.

The challenge is that though there are marker "blenders" which help make color blending easier, you need to have a big set with lots of colors in different values and hues. A handful of colors are usually not enough for the effects you want to achieve. It is very easy to make the sketch too bright and colorful.

Pastels

Pastel is erroneously believed to be the invention of the German landscape painter, Johann Alexander Thiele (1685 - 1752), but it has since been proven that at least Guido Reni, the noted Italian master - who died more than forty years before Thiele was born - had already worked in pastel. This medium is pure powdered pigment, compressed into small, cylindrical sticks. Recently, semi-hard pastels have been introduced. These contain a small amount of wax. The medium didn't become popular until 1775, when pastels by the Swiss artist, Jean Etienne Liotard, were shown at the Royal Academy in London.

There are two kinds of pastels: soft pastels and oil pastels. They are both fine media.

They have the nature and quality of colored pencils but their softness and richness is an additional advantage. I rarely use pastels for theatre design renderings but I do use them for figure drawings and portrait drawings.

Figure 5-9. *Rendering by Wenhai Ma for* Arsenic and Old Lace, *markers over ink sketch, 9¼" x 7" 2011.*

Figure 5-10. *Soft pastels and oil pastels. Photo by Wenhai Ma.*

The challenge is that unless you work on large pieces, it is difficult to get details with pastels because of the size and softness of them. You will need to apply a coat of picture fixative over the sketch to protect the pastel dust when your sketch is finished.

Figure 5-11 and 5-12. *Drawings by Wenhai Ma, soft pastels on brown pastel paper, all 22" x 15" 2003.*

Figure 5-13. *Drawing by Wenhai Ma, oil pastels on brown pastel paper, 22" x 15", 2003.*

6

COLOR MIXING

"There are hidden harmonies or contrasts in colors which involuntarily combine to work together ..."

Vincent Willem van Gogh (1853–1890)
Dutch post-Impressionist painter.

DRAWING BY WENHAI MA

The Color Wheel

The color wheel is a very good tool for us to understand the primary colors, the secondary colors and the tertiary colors mixed from them, including the grays, browns and neutral colors. It shows how the colors are mixed. Colors opposite one another on the color wheel set up dramatic contrasts.

Colors react with each other in two ways: they contrast or harmonize. Color relationship can be explored on the color wheel according to their positions. As you might expect, the colors which harmonize are close to each other, while those that contrast to each other are far apart on the color wheel.

You will also see that the upper half of the color wheel contains the warm colors and the lower half of it contains the cool colors.

Colors of opposite characteristics create impact when they meet as you see from the color wheel. Artists of the Renaissance were fond of light and dark contrast. The Impressionists were fond of contrasts of warm and cool colors and complementary colors.

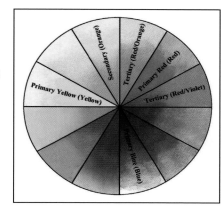

Figure 6-1. *Color wheel created by Wenhai Ma, watercolor and Photoshop.*

Primary Colors

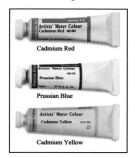

Figure 6-2. *The primary colors, Photoshop sketch by Wenhai Ma.*

The primary colors are the ones that cannot be made by the mixing of any other colors. It is extremely important to have at least the three primary colors: red, blue and yellow. In most of the color sets, especially watercolor sets, these primary colors can be questionable. The red and yellow are mostly acceptable but the blue sometimes is not what should be called "primary blue". It looks more like Cobalt Blue and you cannot obtain a decent green by mixing it with yellow or a decent violet by mixing it with red. The following three colors can be considered as the three primary colors for painter's purposes: Cadmium Red, Prussian Blue and Cadmium Yellow:

Theoretically, any color can be obtained by mixing two or three of the Primary Colors though it is not quite true. Certain bright colors are impossible to be obtained. We have to obtain a couple of additional ready-mixed colors such as Cadmium Lake, Rose Madder, Alizarin Crimson; Winsor Green, or Viridian Hue for a more complete pallet.

Furthermore, there is one more color that I use often: Vandyke Brown or Burnt Umber. I like to use it with Prussian Blue, when Vandyke Brown is served as a "warm" color, while Prussian Blue is served as "cool" color. These two colors make for a harmonious and yet contrasting pallet.

It is very important that you see and read colors astutely, in the same way that a piano tuner must have a good ear for tones, even the slightest differences and inaccuracies. It is simply a matter of commanding your hands to mix the colors while your eyes make judgment, then your hand again making adjustments until you get what you want. I highly encourage you do some color matching exercises simply by imitating colors you see in a piece of artwork. This is a good way to train your color reading comprehension and abilities for mixing colors accurately and quickly.

Figure 6-3. *This is a watercolor set I have been using for most of my renderings and illustrations. Note that the Blue that came with the set is actually NOT "Primary Blue" but rather is Cobalt Blue and therefore, I bought Prussian Blue in an individual tube.*

Figure 6-4. *This is the paint elevation I prepared for a backdrop for* The College Widow, *Purdue University, 2006. I use this as a color matching project for my rendering classes. Note that I did not use any white at all but I watered colors down so the values and hues were adjusted.*

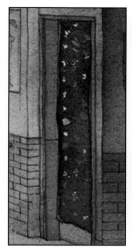

Figure 6-5 and 6-6. *Details from* No.1 Restaurant in China *and illustration from* Red Means Good Fortune, *all by Wenhai Ma, 2002 and 1994. Note that I used white watercolor paint for the door curtain and the snow.*

Occasionally, I use white only for small spots such as stars on a dark background, or white print on a dark color curtain. I do however often use white for picking out highlights.

Markers, colored pencils and water-soluble pencils have similar natures and characteristics of watercolor though there is a limitation in color mixing and blending. You may overlay two or three colors one on top of the other because they are transparent. You may also use a "blender" to mix colors, though it is not as easy and handy as with watercolor.

Acrylic, gouache, soft pastels, oil pastels and oil usually require white for different tones, or lightness, of a color.

Color Mixing

"The hidden harmony is better than the obvious."

Pablo Ruiz Picasso (188–1973)
Spanish painter, draughtsman, and sculptor.

Color Scheme & Tones

Colors affect us in numerous ways, both mentally and physically, and contribute a subliminal role in influencing our desires; like hunger, passion, anger, peace, calm and more. A strong red color has been shown to raise the blood pressure, while a blue color has a calming effect. With colors you can set a mood, atmosphere, attract attention and make a statement, particular in theatre design renderings and paint elevations. Being able to use colors consciously and harmoniously can help you create spectacular results. You can use color to energize, or to cool down. By selecting the right color scheme, you can create an ambiance of elegance, warmth or tranquility, or you can convey an image of playful youthfulness. Color can be your most powerful design element if you learn to use it effectively.

A very important aspect of color is that it is emotive and denotes character. It stimulates our senses and emotions, not just our eyes. As said by Emil Nolde (1867-1956, German painter and printmaker), *"Yellow can express happiness, and then again, pain. There is flame red, blood red and rose red. There is silver blue and thunder blue. Every color harbors its own soul, delighting or disgusting or stimulating me."* Color can suggest and accentuate the mood of a painting, as well as create an emotional response in the mind of viewer and the audience in the theatre. We see the same in films.

Here are some thoughts on the colors:

Primary Color Scheme: Red, Yellow and Blue. These colors are energetic, direct; bold statements can be made.

Secondary Color Scheme: Green, Orange, and Violet. Great for nature scenes. Be careful you don't fall into a boring trap of all green grass and foliage, orange autumn trees and violet mountains.

Tertiary Colors: Tertiary Color Schemes can be composed of two sets. One set is Yellow/Green, Red/Orange and Blue/Violet. The other set will be composed of Yellow/Orange, Red/Violet and Blue/Green. Yellow/Orange will add warm accents and maybe some interesting excitement.

Analogous Colors: This is a no-brainer, they will always be harmonious because they are neighbors, adjacent to each other on the color wheel. They are beautiful through subtle gradation from one color to the next. Imagine them as a family, so start with the "head of the family", one color to dominate, now choose one or even two colors on either side of the "head": Yellow, with Green and Orange.

Harmonic color schemes does not only mean colors in the same picture are varied shades. It also means the colors are related to each other and yet each has its own color tendency. For example, in the picture, there may be reddish red, bluish red, yellowish red, pinkish red, grayish red, and so on. Look at people in the street or in the classroom. Many wear blacks and blues. Are they the same black? No. Are they the same blue? No. Each black or blue has a color tendency and characteristic. A black or blue can be bluish, reddish or yellowish. Study the old masterpieces and even successful graphic designs, and you will find the colors that appear on the pieces are rich but very subtle and simple.

I sometimes also see young designers try to keep their palettes very clean. They may clean and wipe their palettes every once in a while and in the meantime, may try very hard to "create" pretty colors. In fact, the colors they wiped away were pretty, depending on where and how they are placed. It is like piano keys – they all sound good depending on how you play them, the order, the length, the rhythm and the timing.

Think about Mozart, he used the same music notes that we would use but he composed them in the best order, timing and rhythm to create masterpieces!

Look at Rembrandt's work. Most of his works comprise warm brownish color schemes, or as some of my Chinese friends say – "soy sauce" color scheme. But Rembrandt controlled every element so well — the color tendencies, the tones, hues and values, the placement of the colors. All the colors work together to create a harmonious and beautiful piece, just like Mozart's music.

Similar to music, the tones and colors in a painting are like music notes. If you look at works by Rembrandt, Corot, Degas and Monet, you'll find the charm from their quiet statement and harmonious tonality of color, a sense of significance and dignity.

Tone is an essential part of all painting and drawing, especially in achieving the effects of light on subjects. Tonal values are vital if you want to portray form, compose a picture well and express mood and atmosphere, which is precisely what is needed in scene design.

Some Additional Hints

Shadow is not always cool or dark. Shadows can be as color-varied and experimental as the lights.

Don't rush into darks. They are necessary for emphasis, but don't rush into them. Dark spots are established through contrast. Always remember: less is more. Save the darks in your shadows for special accents placed after you have developed the majority of shadow shapes in the middle-value range.

Figure 6-7. *Reproduction of* The Gleaners, *1857, by Jean-François Millet (1814-20, 1875) Musée d'Orsay. Copied by Shuqing Zhai, oil on canvas, 39½" x 29½", 1995. Note the color scheme is quite "brownish". However, the three primary colors (blue, red and yellow) appear harmoniously on the gleaners among the various browns — reddish brown, yellowish brown, orange brown, and so on. The colors contrast with each other and are harmoniously related.*

The following figures and the color charts (with the desaturated tones below the colors) from them are examples showing how the colors work harmoniously yet each keeps its own color tendency.

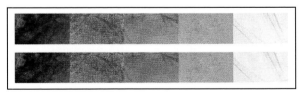

Figures 6-8 through 6-11. *Illustration for* The Painted Fan *by Wenhai Ma, text by Marilyn Singer, a Morrow Junior picture book, 1994. These illustrations show my attempt at creating a greenish-brown color scheme and a brownish grey color scheme with some color contrast accents. Note subtle blues and reds I carefully used, watercolor over pencil lines, 18.5" x 12.5" and 9.25" x 12.25".*

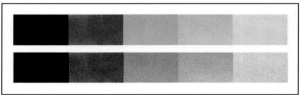

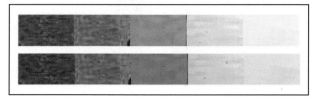

Figures 6-12 and 6-13. *Illustration for* Monkey King Defeats Red Boy *by Wenhai Ma, 2008. Pan Asian Publications, USA. Watercolor and India ink.*

Figures 6-14 and 6-15. *Illustration for* The Fairy *by Wenhai Ma. Text by Charles Perrault. Cobblestone Publishing.*

Though they were done with oil, in *Figures 6-16* through *6-31* that follow the watercolor scheme arrangement is actually the same as oil, and all other media.

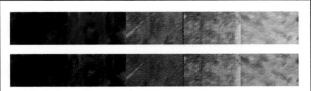

Figures 6-16 and 6-17. *Artwork by Wenhai Ma, oil on canvas.*

Figures 6-18 and 6-19. *Artwork by Wenhai Ma, oil on board.*

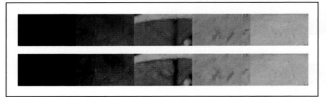

Figures 6-20 and 6-21. *Artwork by Wenhai Ma, oil on canvas.*

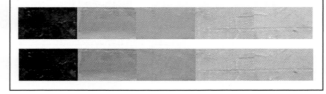

Figures 6-22 and 6-23. *Artwork by Wenhai Ma, oil on board.*

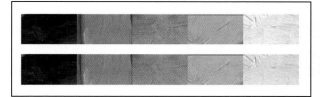

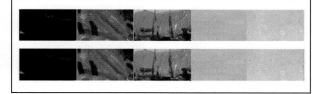

Figures 6-24 and 6-25. *Artwork by Wenhai Ma, oil on board.*

Figures 6-26 and 6-27. *Artwork by Wenhai Ma, oil on board.*

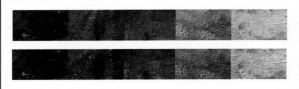

Figures 6-28 and 6-29. *Artwork by Wenhai Ma, oil on canvas.*

Figures 6-30 and 6-31. *Artwork by Wenhai Ma, oil on board.*

Paint on the Palette

When I paint with oil and gouache, I like to arrange my palette with colors from light to dark and from white to black, with the transitional colors in between: white, the yellow colors, the green colors, the red colors, the purple colors, the blue colors, the gray colors and black. This may serve as a handy and inspirational sequence when picking up colors and balancing the color scheme. I use more colors when I work with oil and gouache but a lot less with watercolor.

As for watercolor, the arrangement is similar, except there is no white put on the palette. When white is needed, it can be put on a separate palette or container, in order to avoid messing it up with other colors. Any color mixed with white will lose transparency and become opaque.

Unless you use a palette with paint block pans, you may arrange your palette in this order, as shown in *Figure 6-32*.

- Ivory Black, or Lamp Black
- Prussian Blue, or Phthalocyanine Blue
- Scarlet, or Cadmium Red
- Lemon Yellow, or Yellow Light
- Crimson Lake, or Rose Madder Alizarin
- Green Deep, or Viridian Hue
- Van Dyke Brown, or Burnt Umber

In watercolor, I do not include white on my palette. I prefer to use a separate palette or a container, or simply a piece of paper as a palette. It is because white makes the color opaque, dull and muddy if my brush touches it accidentally. It will then not look like watercolor but like gouache. Thus, I am always very careful with white. I even replace my water jars with clean fresh water after rinsing my brush with white in it.

When white is needed, you may use either the watercolor white, or gouache white.

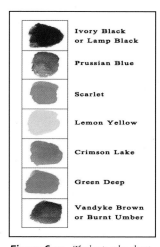

Figure 6-32. *The basic color chart for watercolor – this will be sufficient for most of your needs. Photoshop-aided photo by Wenhai Ma. Lots of people arrange their palettes similarly. You don't have to do it this way if you have your own habit and system, as long as you feel comfortable and you master your palette well.*

I do not use Cobalt Blue unless it is absolutely necessary. Probably the only time I would ever use it is when I work on oriental decorative projects that require that specific color.

Certain colors, such as Crimson Lake and Prussian Blue, once accidentally spilled can be very tough to remove. If a chunk of paint is not mixed well it may stain the paper. Therefore you should pay more attention to those colors and mix them well before applying.

Limit Your Palette

Though there are so many colors available, we tend to have a shortlist of favorite colors that we prefer to have on our palette. When painting with watercolors, you probably have six to eight colors you use on a regular basis. At times, we find we can paint with a few standard colors or use a limited paint palette. Nevertheless, even these can be narrowed down to achieve stunning color effects.

It is interesting to approach a theatre design rendering with a limited palette. An artist will choose as few colors as possible to add to their palette and mix the rest of the needed colors from this limited color palette. This helps to remove some of the palette confusion and riot of colors that can often produce muddy colors and challenge the artist and painting.

It is a challenge for designers to simplify their works and to loosen up. A limited palette is a good step to help reduce the temptation of adding unnecessary extra colors which may confuse the artwork. Adding a color doesn't mean that it adds measurable results to your artwork. Try working with as few colors as you can and see the results you can obtain.

You may find historical palettes used by Titian, Goya, Renoir, Rubens, Pissarro, Cezanne and more art masters. Each artist seems to have found a limited set of favorite colors they used on a regular basis to create their master works of art.

Begin with One Color

To begin with, what are the right colors to work with or add to a limited palette? Of course, your reference materials or subject has a significant input on your color choice. An under-painting for your work will often begin as a tonal (monochromatic) or one-color rendering of your subject. Even though only one color is used, the transparency of different colors or the use of media will allow you to create different values or lights and darks. Under-paintings created with this approach are often beautiful works of art and can stand on their own.

This is also an efficient method to figure out the shadow and light effect. It may also help you figure out certain watercolor techniques. I recommend trying Vandyke Brown, as it will give you that great sepia look.

Figure 6-33. *Rendering by Wenhai Ma for* The Bald Soprano *by Eugene Ionesco, watercolor, white gouache and white pencil on pencil sketch and pasted photo collage, 12 ½" x 9", 1982.*

Two-Color Rendering

Other colors are often added that are not easy to mix but might be required by the subject. This limited palette may be extended to include greens, oranges and reds where the hue, chroma and intensity of the color is not easily obtained by combining the limited colors in the palette.

If you add a second color — Prussian Blue in addition to the first color Vandyke Brown — your color palette will look richer. You need to place them well so Vandyke Brown works on the "warm color" side while Prussian Blue works on the "cool color" side. If you mix these two, in different proportions and different hues, your palette will become a lot richer.

Figure 6-34. *Rendering by Wenhai Ma for* The Tempest, *Duke University. Colors used: Prussian Blue, Vandyke Brown, 7 ½" x 3 ½", 1997.*

Add a Third Color

Then you may add a third color on your palette: Yellow Light. Yellow Light is also on the "warm color" side. Because of the sunny, radiant nature of this color, it will make your palette a great deal warmer and more vivid. It also represents light. Other than Yellow Light, Crimson Lake or Orange are also good options, depending on your design and the color scheme you want to achieve.

Figure 6-35. *Rendering by Wenhai Ma for* Macbeth, *The Duke Stage Company, watercolor. Colors used: Prussian Blue, Vandyke Brown and Yellow Light over Photoshop edited and printed pencil sketch. 10" x 7 ¼".*

Add a Fourth and Fifth Color

The fourth color I would suggest is green, particularly when the scene involves lots of trees and bushes, etc. However, you'll need to be careful with the color green. When we portray trees, we tend to think that the leaves are green while branches are brown. In fact this is not the case. If you hold a true green color in front of tree leaves, you'll find the green you have should be toned down and adjusted – to be mixed with something else, perhaps some brown or orange. With the added fourth color, your palette becomes a whole lot richer.

Figure 6-36. *Rendering for* Full Moon, *Duke University. Set and costume designed by Wenhai Ma, watercolor and India ink, 10" x 7", 1987. Colors used: Prussian Blue, Vandyke Brown, Yellow Light and Crimson Lake.*

7

RENDERING WITH WATERCOLOR

On painting a watercolor ...

"Make the best of an emergency."

John Singer Sargent (1856–1925)
American portait painter and watercolorist.

DRAWING BY WENHAI MA

Watercolor is a tricky medium to master. Young designers may even fear watercolor to begin with. However there is nothing to fear. It is better to make mistakes and learn some fundamentals, embrace the challenge and get started. At worst you may produce unsuccessful renderings with muddy colors and flat, opaque values. I did exactly the same years ago when I first started at Carnegie Mellon. I've learned a great deal and produced some good renderings since. Watercolor is a medium that requires planning, timing, control over the water in your brush and some other special skills. Unlike acrylic and gouache, once you have a mistake or accident on paper, it is impossible to fix it. However, it is really worth having these skills in your repertoire. An artist may spend a lifetime exploring materials, techniques and the different results each can achieve. You will discover the unique characteristics and advantages and you'll love it!

In the earlier period, the transparency of watercolor paint was emphasized. In "pure" watercolor painting, or the "English Method," no white is used. Instead, patches or spots of white paper are left untouched to depict white areas and reflected light. The paper itself acts as the white, while water is the medium. Different hues are obtained by varying the quantity of water in your brush. Thus, de Wint or Turner see watercolor as a kind of fluid, lightly-tinted sketch. Color tones and atmospheric effects are achieved by staining the paper with varying amounts of color pigments, called "washes."

There is usually a "White" included in your watercolor set, either in a pan or a tube. I strongly suggest that you put it away and do not touch it. Instead, get used to using water to tone colors down and use the paper itself to represent your white values. Furthermore, to avoid getting the color opaque and muddy, make sure that there is no white paint kept on the palette. You might accidentally touch the white paint and mix it with other colors.

It is true that to make a good rendering takes time and good planning. I believe all of these are necessary for young designers. However, after some practice, experimentation, frustration and success, you will streamline and simplify the process.

The Challenges

Watercolor permits and facilitates dropping color into wet washes to produce color blends, flows and blooms impossible in other media. It is heavily weighted toward technique and control. Learned skill is instantly evident in the work. Because it is more difficult, it is appreciated more.

The most challenging aspects in watercoloring are the control of the quantity in the brush, the timing and the impact the paper has, how the paint spreads (or doesn't) depending on how damp the paper is. These traits are what make watercolor challenging but also what make it unique.

The Temperature

Temperature affects watercolors. It is recommended that you spend a little time to understand the climatic conditions in your region.

In a dry climate your watercolor paper dries faster and therefore it makes certain effects you want difficult to obtain. You may need to do some experiments and tests and make sure you have good control of the timing, and get an idea of the water quantity in your brush. You'll certainly need a bit more water in your brush and to work a bit faster in this climate.

In a humid region it may take quite a while for watercolor paper to dry. You can use a hair dryer to dry sections of the piece as you're coloring. But you don't want to turn the hair dryer up high, no matter how impatient you are, because you don't want the water evaporating or to overheat the paper. Don't put the hair dryer close to the paper. Keep it at least a foot away from the surface.

Put the hair dryer on its lowest setting, and wave it back and forth across the paper to ensure it dries evenly. You don't want one part to dry out before another, as the sheet may then buckle. If you're working on unstretched paper, use the hair dryer on the back of the sheet as well as the front. If you find yourself getting too impatient to wait for a watercolor to dry, try working on the dry areas or do something else instead.

I prefer to do my watercolor in an environment with a certain amount of humidity so I am allowed to take my time to obtain the wet-in-wet effect I want.

Appreciate Colors on Your Palette – "Gorgeous Greys"

You may have discovered that grey colors or tones can be attractive and you'll get varied assortments when you mix variations in hue. Grey and natural hues can be made by combining nearly equal amounts of the three primary colors in a triad.

Try to limit your palette, though you must have the correct three primary colors at least. Try to utilize the colors on your palette well. To share a "secret" with you: I never clean or wash my palette — I finish up all the paint I put on it, even sometimes when the colors seem dull, grey and dirty. As long as I place them harmoniously, they will add something to my scene.

Figure 7-1. *Subtle variations of neutrals mixed by the three primary colors. The grey tones can be beautiful. Watercolor by Wenhai Ma.*

Flat Wash

This is the first basic watercolor skill to learn. Take some time and learn to paint flat washes, such as the sky, without any overlapping marks created when you add new color. Depending on each individual project, I usually work this way:

If the sky area is light enough and the color will go well with the rest of the color scheme, I would dampen (do not leave too much water on the paper) the whole paper with my 3" flat brush, and using the same brush, loaded with lots of paint, color across the area in as few strokes as possible. Let it dry, then work on the other areas and objects on top of the sky. The thin sky color under the objects will not be recognized. It may help unify the color scheme, kind of like when you look at things through sunglasses.

The Wet-in-Wet Technique

This is an exciting exercise in the free-flowing possibilities of watercolor. Practiced often, it is a fun, expressive and beautiful watercolor painting technique. When colors are applied to a piece of damp watercolor paper or an area with wet paint, they run out over the wet surface making a unique soft and hazy edge to the colored shape.

Wet your watercolor paper. Before it dries, apply or drop a color onto it from your brush. You'll see the color bleeds, like sun rays. This technique is particularly effective in portraying dramatic atmosphere in theatre design rendering, producing gentle gradations of tone with interesting misty lighting effects. I usually use this technique for the first one or two steps when working on a scene design rendering.

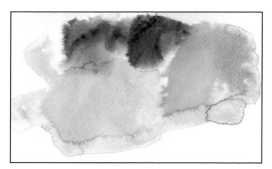  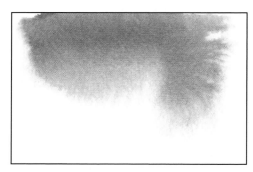

Figures 7-2 and 7-3. *When colors are applied directly onto wet watercolor paper, they run and bleed softly.*

Figure 7-4. *When the board is tilted at an angle of about 30 degrees after coloring, the color flows gently down the paper.*

The Wet-on-Dry Techniques

This traditional technique is used for building up a series of transparent layers, one over the other. Each layer of wash is allowed to dry before the next is layered on top of it. This technique is usually used for portraying details, defined shades and shadows in theatre rendering. The dry surface of paper "holds" the color so the brush strokes will be in control and do not run out and bleed.

Working on Details and Fine Spots

When working on details and fine spots such as actors, furniture, shadows, wallpaper, steps, and window frames, highlights on actors and on scenic elements, etc, I recommend you use a fine-pointed brush. Try to keep as little paint in the brush as possible. Hold the brush up straight and work carefully. Turn the paper around for the best convenient position when you work on these details.

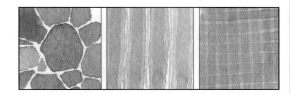

Figures 7-5 through 7-7. *Illustration from* The Japanese Theatre *and* The Sun Catcher *by Wenhai Ma, watercolor on paper.*

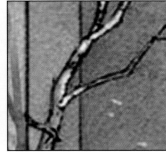

Figures 7-8 and 7-9. *Note the fine details I portrayed with my No. 2 round watercolor brush.*

Creating Highlights

Most young designers or less experienced watercolorists tend to color every part of the paper with paint. This is actually not necessary and even undesirable. The paper itself provides a unique and brilliant white which can be used to great effect and add additional sparkles to your colors — allow the painting to "breathe." There are some techniques that are used to manipulate the paint to create highlights. See *Figure 7-10.*

Figure 7-10. *Left to right: Reserving the highlights; using white paint; using white pencil; masking out.*

Mist, Fog and Smoke Effects

I usually use an old toothbrush and a piece of cardboard to spatter white gouache or watercolor to create mist. Being opaque, the white will show up on top of the watercolor you've already put down. Remember, however, it needs to be a very thin wash so it doesn't totally obscure what you've painted or look unrealistic, so experiment on another sheet of paper before doing it on your finished piece.

Mist is best done at one time by the "wet-in-wet technique" though this requires very careful planning and control. Again, you must test it out before you go to the actual sketch. You may use Photoshop to create the mist effect over a scanned sketch and use it as a reference.

"Happy Accidents"

Unlike using other media, when using watercolor you may make "accidents" or "mistakes." Decide whether it really is an accident or whether it adds an unexpected effect to the painting. Consider letting the painting go in its own direction rather than forcing your preconceived ideas on it — you may end up appreciating the "accidents" and take advantage of the unexpected effects. I recommend you play with the colors on paper and get to know them

Figure 7-11. *Mist effect created by using the wet-in-wet technique. Illustration for* Monkey King Wreaks Havoc in Heaven *by Wenhai Ma. Pan Asian Publications, USA.*

well. When accidents happen, don't panic and try to get things fixed immediately. Just wait till that area dries up and work on other areas. Eventually, you may like these accidents and call them "happy accidents!"

If you make a mistake in a watercolor painting, you either need to react fast and remove it almost instantaneously, before it's had time to soak into the paper, or wait for the painting to dry completely. If the paint doesn't come off in one go, don't scrub with the brush on the paper as you're likely to damage it. Rather, leave the watercolor to dry and then repeat the process. (See Chapter 4, pp. 82-83)

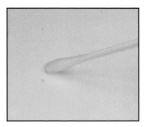

Figure 7-12. *Using a Q-tip to remove an accidental ink spot.*

Salt Texture Effects

The salt texture effect can only be obtained with watercolor. The iodized table salt we normally use for cooking will work well. Apply a color wash to the paper. Let the color wash stay on the paper for a minute or so. Spread a few light dustings of salt crystals into the colored area. Leave it flat till it dries. Dust the salt away. You'll find that the salt grains absorbed the paint and left an unexpected unique texture like snow flakes.

Figure 7-13. *Details of an illustration for* **Swan's Gift** *by Wenhai Ma, text by Brenda Seabrooke, a Candlewick Press book, 14" x 22", watercolor and India ink on paper, 1995. The splatters were created by the salt texture technique.*

The salt technique is a one-time technique. You need to make sure the paint you apply on paper is strong and dark enough, and the density what you want to end up with. Even when the salt technique area is dry, you may not want to work on it, especially to smudge your wet brush on the area, for it will flatten the salt effect and brush your paint away. You cannot repeat the technique over and over again on the same area. The paper will not react the same as when it was fresh and untouched. This technique can be very tricky. You should have things well planned before doing it. Some practice and experiment will help you understand the reaction and the effect you may get. The salt texture effect is usually ideal for representing dream or fantasy scenes.

 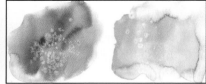

Figure 7-14 and 7-15. *Using table salt for unique watercolor texture effects.*

Masking/Blocking Techniques

Masking Fluid

Masking fluid (or frisket) comes in a bottle. It is the most common medium to mask off part of the rendering. It's a solution of latex in ammonia and may be removed by gently rubbing it off, either with your fingers or an eraser, once the painting is dry. Use your dip pen or brush to apply a thin coat on the needed spot or use a brush on a larger area to mask it. The fluid takes a couple of minutes to dry. Then you can simply color on top of it as if it does not exist. You may also block out areas that have already been colored and apply another layer of color on top.

Your dip pen allows you draw lines or block small areas, while your brush allows you to cover large areas. You need to have your pen or brush cleaned up immediately after use or the fluid may block the nib of the pen or stick in the bristles and damage your brush. It's advisable to apply masking fluid with an old brush or one kept solely for this purpose. Some artists recommend dipping a brush in dishwashing liquid before you use masking fluid, as this makes it easier to wash out of a brush. Other than a pen and a brush, you may use a toothpick to dip the fluid and tap it on the planned spots if they are small.

You'll find the blocked area is kept as a clean, untouched spot. If you find it too clean, you may also apply some thin wash, though you need to make sure to blend the wash with the surroundings. To do this, you may like to dampen an area larger than you need, but do not apply paint all way to the edge so it gradually fades out with an almost invisible edge.

Masking fluid which has color in it is easier to use than one which is white or transparent as you can see where you've applied it.

Rubber cement can also be used as a masking medium though you should test it out and see how it works before applying it to the actual rendering sketch surface.

You can buy an "eraser" made from crepe rubber specifically for removing masking fluid. Using one instead of your fingers to remove masking fluid has the advantage that you don't accidentally transfer grease or paint from your fingers onto your painting.

Permanent masking fluid is a special type of masking fluid, formulated to be left on the paper permanently.

Figure 7-16. *Masking fluid and brushes. Photo created by Wenhai Ma.*

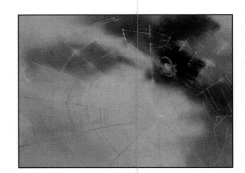

Figure 7-17. *Details of an illustration for* The Sun Catcher *by Wenhai Ma. Note the spider web was obtained by using the masking fluid technique.*

Frisket Film or Masking Tape

Frisket film is a clear, low-tack masking film that can be used to mask out areas of a painting. You cut it to shape and stick it down on your painting. Ensure that the edges are stuck down so paint doesn't seep in underneath it.

You may also use masking tape instead of frisket film to block small areas. Look at the "glowing moon" effect in *Figure 7-19*. It was done by the following steps:

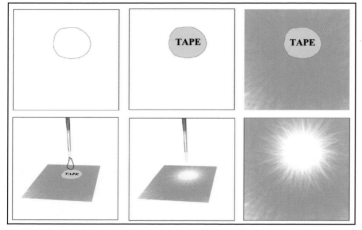

Figure 7-19. *Left to right and top to bottom: Draw the spot that you will block with tape; Cut a piece of masking tape to the shape and size of the moon and stick it on the spot; Apply a couple of brush strokes on the dampened paper surface and let it bleed; Before it dries up, drop a clean drop of water from the brush right on the taped moon; The water drop washes the paint away on the background; Peel the tape away from the moon when the paper is dry and the moon glows!*

The Wax and Crayon Resist Techniques

You may use a candle or a wax crayon to scribble over clean paper and color over this area as you normally do. You'll get an unexpected texture. I occasionally use this technique for rain drops, stars, the Moon, etc.

Figure 7-18. *Dedication spot for* Swan's Gift *by Wenhai Ma, text by Brenda Seabrooke, a Candlewick Press book, 1995. Note the bleeding technique I used for the grey background and the moon. Watercolor, pencil and India ink, 3" x 3", approximately.*

Figure 7-20. *A white crayon. Photo by Wenhai Ma.*

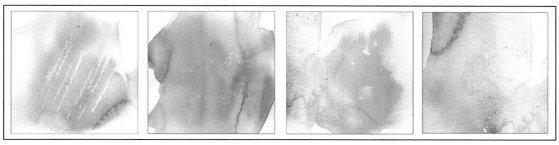

Figure 7-21. *The white lines and the white dots were drawn before coloring. The crayon strokes blocked the paper and left the lines as rain drops and the dots as stars.*

The Brushwork

The two most common brushwork techniques are the wet-in-wet technique and wet on dry technique as seen in Figure 7-22.

Figure 7-22. *Different brushes, different strokes, and different effects. Mostly the wet-in-wet and wet on dry techniques were used for depicting the misty atmosphere in the mountains. Illustration by Wenhai Ma for* Lost on a Mountain in Maine. *Watercolor and India ink.*

Techniques, Effects and Tricks

The two charts below include most of the techniques and effects in water coloring.

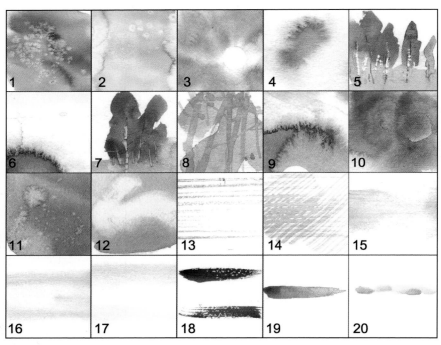

Figure 7-23. *1 and 2: Using salt; 3: The moon was blocked by masking tape, the wash done by the wet-in-wet technique; 4: The wet-in-wet technique; 5: The wet on dry technique. The tree trunks were scratched in by an X-acto knife blade; 6: The effect was obtained by applying the wet on dry stroke and then a clear water stroke right around the color stroke; 7: The tree trunks were scraped using a toothpick; 8: The dry on dry technique; 9: The moon was blocked by masking tape, then the wet-in-wet technique; 10: The wet-in-wet technique with alcohol drops; 11: Those "stars" were obtained by using a toothpick, with a tiny bit of clear water on the tip each time; 12: I got the stroke by using a clean damp brush, on the color wash while it was still wet; 13: This stroke was obtained by using a dry fan brush; 14: After the dry fan brush stroke dried, I applied another stroke in a different direction; 15: Dry fan brush stroke into wet paper; 16: Subtle brush strokes over wet paper; 17: Wet strokes with different colors into wet paper; 18: Dry brush strokes from left to right and from right to left, with an interesting texture obtained; 19: I got this stroke with heavy paint at first. I added water in the brush and continued on the same stroke; 20: I started with a clear water stroke and added different color while it was damp.*

Figure 7-24. **21:** *Bold and firm strokes, wet on dry technique;* **22:** *Heavily-loaded paint, firm stroke;* **23:** *Heavily-loaded paint, half on dry paper, half on damp paper;* **24:** *Heavily-loaded brush stroke continued with a clear water stroke;* **25:** *Dry brush stroke;* **26:** *Very dry fan brush stroke;* **27:** *Heavily-loaded brush, rolled from left to right;* **28:** *Dry brush strokes create a firm and strong sense;* **29:** *I used a very dry old round watercolor brush for the grass;* **30:** *The stroke was erased by using an eraser after the wet on dry stroke got dry;* **31:** *Wet-into-wet with clear water drops while it was damp;* **32:** *The texture was obtained by using a dry fan brush when the strokes were still damp;* 33: *The texture was obtained by using a hair comb when the paint was still damp;* **34 and 35:** *Bi-colored fan brush stroke into wet paper;* **36:** *Bi-colored fan brush stroke;* **37:** *Wet into very wet paper surface;* **38:** *The light beams were obtained by the wet-into-wet and wet on dry techniques;* **39:** *This misty and moody light beam was obtained by the wet-into-wet technique;* **40:** *This stroke obtained by the wet-into-wet technique can be used on the stage floor, suggesting the spot light effect.*

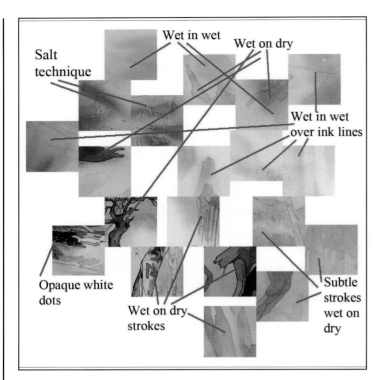

Salt technique

Wet in wet

Wet on dry

Wet in wet over ink lines

Opaque white dots

Wet on dry strokes

Subtle strokes wet on dry

Figure 7-25. *This chart shows various watercolor techniques applied to actual artworks (Details). All by Wenhai Ma.*

Figure 7-26. *Illustration by Wenhai Ma. Watercolor and India ink. Note that there was no white used. The whites are obtained by contrasting the unpainted areas with the neighboring colors.*

Figures 7-27 to 31. *Note that these watercolor figures were mainly portrayed with shadow and light though occasionally the "contour lines" are kept and stressed. Watercolor on paper over pencil sketch by Wenhai Ma, 2004-05.*

Varnishing

Varnish is more than simply a layer to protect your artwork from pollution in the atmosphere and abrasion. It will also bring out the colors to the brilliance they had when you applied them.

Ensure your rendering is completely dry. Use a flat bristle brush to apply the varnish. With the rendering flat, work from the top to the bottom, applying the varnish in parallel strokes from one edge of the rendering to the other. Always work in the same direction. When the first coat of varnish is dry, apply a second coat at right angles to the first. This will give you a good, even finish. Leave the rendering flat for at least ten minutes after you've finished varnishing to stop the varnish running down the painting.

To test whether the varnish is dry or not, touch the edge of the rendering to see if it's still tacky. It should dry within a couple of hours, depending on the weather. Always varnish the whole of the rendering in one go. If you do only a part and this has started to dry before you do the rest, you'll end up with a line where the first part ends. Try to have the same amount of varnish on the brush for each stroke so you put equal amounts of varnish on all parts of the rendering. Work in a dust-free environment, otherwise dust particles will get stuck in the wet varnish. Varnish will soak into the paper and therefore does not allow your watercolor technique to work if you want to color over it. A high-quality product is highly recommended for varnishing. All Purpose Varnish Spray is also a good option.

Other Watercolor Media

There are other media that may be used in watercoloring to help create special effects:

Aqua Pasto is a gel medium which thickens washes and provides texture.

Gum Arabic increases paint transparency and gloss.

Ox gall improves the flow of washes over hard papers.

Workshop I

This is a rendering for an original Chinese musical, *Crazy Snow*, portraying the moment when there was a big crowd of chorus and ensemble on the stage. The musical was based on a true story during the Anti-Japanese Invasion War. On the stage, there is a turntable 54 feet in diameter. On top of it there are platforms operated by a mechanical hydraulic system, with scenic pieces representing destroyed town houses and homes serving as legs and borders. There are barbed wire, remaining shop signs and lots of smoke. It is a war scene. I chose a grayish umber color scheme for this rendering, with some red light coming from stage left representing fire – the burning land.

Remember: watercolor is tricky. Particularly when you work with the wet-in-wet technique, it is very important to concentrate. You'll need to make sure that you will not be interrupted or disturbed while working.

You Will Need

Brushes: I personally tend to use my own Chinese watercolor brush called "Medium White Cloud", though you may absolutely use a regular watercolor brush #8. You will also need a wide, soft flat brush for wetting the paper and coloring large areas. The one I usually use is called "Brush FLT SHT HN".

Watercolor palette: You will need to have some paint mixed, ready to be used. I personally like to start with Prussian Blue and Vandyke Brown, so I usually squeeze these colors apart on my palette and mix a third color from these two in a small dish, ready for use. Let's call this color "bluish brown".

Two containers with fresh water: You will always need to have a container of clean water in case you may need to wash away a stroke or an accident.

A hair dryer: It'll help you to speed up when you work with a "dry color" technique.

Kitchen paper towel: for cleaning your brush. It also helps you to control the quantity of water in your brush.

Figure 7-32. *We are revisiting this figure because it shows the work station with the most needed references particularly for this rendering: the shadow & light study sketch, the color scheme study sketch and the supplies and tools.*

Figure 7-33. *Colored model for* **Crazy Snow,** *1cm : 25cm. Notice that the HL is rather high because I wanted to show the platforms on the stage floor. It is also a good idea to place the color model nearby as a color and texture reference.*

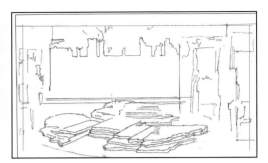

Figure 7-34. *Traced sketch from printed model photo, ink pen on tracing paper, 10½" x 6¾".*

Figure 7-35. *Pencil in the details and actors over enlarged photocopy, 10½" x 6¾".*

Figure 7-36. *Traced sketch on watercolor paper, Arches, 140 lb, 16½" x 10". Note that I refined the traced sketch to give it a vivid sketch quality rather than a directly traced cartoon. I applied some sketchy pencil strokes for the surround to add some atmospheric quality. I used a T-square to check some of the vertical and horizontal lines. I mainly used an H pencil because soft pencil strokes might otherwise be washed away when coloring.*

Figure 7-37. *Shadow and light study sketch, 2B pencil over photocopied sketch, 7" x 5". In this step, I figured out the lighting effect I wanted for my rendering. I used a small piece of rolled-up toilet tissue to smudge on certain areas and an eraser to pick up the highlights. On this sketch I also built up the atmosphere.*

Figure 7-38. *Photoshop rendering over scanned pencil sketch. I find this step is quite helpful for I can get the color scheme figured out easily, so I should be quite confident when I color in the actual pencil sketch on watercolor paper. Like the pencil shadow and light study sketch, it is a good reference. Certainly this color study sketch can be done by hand.*

Figure 7-39. *Now you see I put tape pieces on the back of the pencil sketch on watercolor paper.*

Figure 7-40. *A well-prepared line sketch on watercolor paper ready for coloring, taped on the drawing board. I simply used masking tape this time. Note that my drawing board is actually a piece of plywood made of fine white birch, not anything "plastic". Remember that plastic or man-made materials do not absorb water so if you do not have a proper drawing board, you may have to cover your board with a piece of drawing paper so it helps absorb the water – simply tape it down with masking tape.*

Figure 7-41. *My work station. Note that I mainly used two brushes for this rendering: a brush FLT SHT HN and the "Medium White Cloud" – both have bristles made of soft goat hair. In the palette on the upper right corner, I prepared three watered-down colors: 1. brownish orange, mixed by Cadmium Orange and Yellow Ochre, 2. reddish brown, mixed by Van Dyke Brown and Cadmium Red Lt., 3. brownish blue, mixed by Van Dyke Brown and Prussian Blue. I believed that those three colors mixed by myself should serve this particular rendering well. It is also a good idea to keep a spare piece of watercolor paper (the same kind as you are using for the actual rendering) handy so you may test the color before applying it to the actual surface.*

Step 1

Figure 7-42. *I wet the paper with the Brush FLT SHT HN, as if I would paint the whole paper with water. Do not leave too much water on the paper, just as long as the paper is damp.*

Step 2

Figure 7-43. *I created the basic atmospheric sense by using my "Medium White Cloud". (A #8 round brush serves the same purpose.) I applied the first strokes with the "bluish brown" when the paper was damp.* This seems to be the most "fearful" stage of all! *I wanted the first few strokes to have a confident, firm, graceful quality. I wanted the color to bleed perfectly. I wanted to show the light, the smoke, the mood and the energy. In this case, the prepared shadow & light study sketch and the color scheme study sketch became very helpful. There is a Chinese saying that can be literally translated as* "possess the matured bamboos in the chest" *when we paint bamboos – meaning "to have a card up one's sleeve" or to have a well thought-out strategy. These sketches, particularly the color study sketch, will serve as* "matured bamboos in the chest". *Hints: You should not overwork this step. Let the paper dry – you may either wait and do something else, or use your hair dryer to speed the process up. However, you should wait for a couple of minutes before using the hair dryer on your work as it might blow the paint in a direction that is not desired. If you have the patience to wait or the time to do something else, I recommend you do not use the dryer to "speed up" things.*

Step 3

Figure 7-44. Work on shadows and different dark shades on the scenic pieces and elements so the light areas begin to show stronger contrast. In this scene, I wanted to portray the scenic elements under different levels of light and colors, in contrast to the background and the neighboring environmental conditions. Again, keep the contrast. Do not overwork on focused spots.

Figure 7-45 and 7-46. I spent some time working on the details mainly with Vandyke Brown and Prussian Blue. I darkened the proscenium arch to get the scene framed and bring in more contrast. Note that I used a bit of subtle Crimson Red and Lemon Yellow on one side of the guard booth on rear stage left to obtain a fire light effect while a bit of subtle Prussian Blue on the other side of the booth and the roof to obtain a color contrast. I used a #6 "Taklon Round Majestic" round brush to work on the details – the actors, the barbed wire horses. I also used the same brush picking up and reinforcing the back light around some of the actors with Titanium White gouache.

Step 4

Figure 7-47. I checked and adjusted the color contrast – warm and cool colors. I checked and adjusted shadow and light contrast – the black and white levels. Make sure not to overwork the rendering– remember, a good artist knows when to stop. 16 ½" x 10", 2005.

Workshop II

This is a design I did for *Hamlet* by Shakespeare produced by Duke University. The rendering portrays the scene of the play-within-the-play. I wanted to create a "greyish-purple" color scheme with strong dramatic and atmospheric lighting effect. Again, I wanted to place the contrast between shadow and light in variations. I wanted to bring some sense of mysterious quality to this scene. Since some of the steps are very much similar to those stated in the previous workshop, I will just omit some of the details and skip a couple of repeated steps.

Step 1

Figure 7-48. *Besides having my well-prepared pencil/ink sketch on watercolor paper taped on my drawing board, I also prepared this color study sketch with Photoshop.*

Step 2

Figure 7-49. *I wet the paper and created the basic atmospheric sense with a couple of brush strokes using my "Medium White Cloud" brush (or a #8 round watercolor brush) when the paper was damp. I mainly used the grayish purple wash with some variations for these strokes.*

Step 3

Figure 7-50. *I let the paper dry. I then wet the paper again and balanced the overall atmospheric sense by applying more strokes with the grayish purple. I varied the colors by adding a slight amount of bluer tone or a slightly browner tone, or even a bit more of a greener tone. This was actually planned on my color scheme study sketch. Always keep the lit and focused areas bright and clean – keep the contrast. In this scene, I wanted to keep the spot on where the Players play the murder scene. I waited for the paper to dry. I then worked on some details such as the actors, the rug, and the show drop. I unified and focused the lighting.*

Step 4

Figure 7-51. *Finished rendering by Wenhai Ma for the play-within-the-play scene for* **Hamlet**, *14"x11". I worked on the characters, props and details. I spent time unifying, adjusting, balancing the shadow and light and wrapped up. I felt that certain spots on my rendering were not dark or strong enough, while certain spots seemed too dark. I used a wet clean brush to wash away certain levels of the paint and reinforce the lines when the surface dried up. Though you may use white to highlight some small areas such as stars, lamp lights, highlights around the characters, etc., since this is a watercolor piece you really cannot rely on white. Your rendering may get quite opaque, muddy and messy. For certain fine lines, you may also use a white pencil instead.*

Then, it was time for me to remove my rendering from the drawing board. Be patient and peel the tape very carefully or the sketch may get ripped!

Pen, Brush and Pencil Stroke Directions

The following figures will show you the tools I used for the rendering for *Hamlet*, the play-within-the-play scene – the moment when the Players came to the castle to prepare the performance.

Figure 7-52. *Sketch traced on 140 lb watercolor paper, 0.3 mechanical pencil.*

Figure 7-53. *Sketch reinforced, lines refined. 0.3 mechanical pencil.*

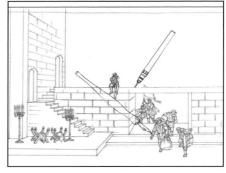

Figure 7-54. *Sketch reinforced with a 0.3 graphic fountain pen and a dip pen. Sepia India ink.*

Figure 7-55. *The "atmospheric strokes," wet-in-wet technique. Note the directions of the brush strokes. Brush: "Medium White Cloud", or #8 round watercolor brush. Colors: Prussian Blue, Van Dyke Brown and Crimson Lake.*

Figure 7-56. *Work on the details: the actors, steps, furniture, chandelier, archways, etc. Reinforce the contrast. Brushes: #2 round watercolor brush and "Medium White Cloud," or #8 round watercolor brush. New color: Yellow Light mixed with Crimson Lake for the steps and furniture. Note the tunnel has been glazed with a thin Crimson Lake wash.*

Figure 7-57. *Renderings by Wenhai Ma for* **Hamlet** *by Shakespeare, Duke University, 1998, watercolor, India ink and pencil, 14" x 11".*

RENDERING WITH ACRYLIC

"The great way to paint with acrylic is the very old-fashioned method of glazing with washes – which you can do with acrylics, of course, marvelously."

David Hockney (born 1937)
English painter, draughtsman, printmaker, stage designer and photographer.

DRAWING BY WENHAI MA

Rohm & Haas, an American firm, started experimenting with acrylic in the 1920s. A group of painters mainly in Mexico started using acrylics for large murals. The artists were aware of the inability of oil paints and frescos to stand up to outdoor weather conditions and were eager to solve the problem. By the mid-1930s artists and scientists worked together and a revolutionary medium was born. However, acrylic was not warmly welcomed in the United States until the 1950s. The new medium was already available and widely used in Europe.

Acrylic, gouache and oil — these three media have a lot in common and among the three, acrylic seems to be the most popular medium for the theatre designer. Acrylic colors are bright and stay the same once dry. Acrylic can also be used to create a "watercolor" effect. Acrylic can imitate both oil paint and watercolor. Many of the old techniques can be adapted to the new medium.

Acrylic can be watered down and worked transparently, somewhat as watercolor, though most of the time, it is used as "paint" – with white added when it needs to be toned down, since the superiority and advantage of acrylic is its opaque nature and its brightness of color.

Acrylic's opaque nature also allows you to use it in a similar fashion to oil paint. It can also be built up with chunky paint and "sculpted" by a palette knife as we do with oil. Paint can be squeezed on and it can also be scraped onto the surface. You may use a plastic card to drag paint thinly across the surface. The greater rigidity of a paint scraper makes thicker and irregular coverage easier to build up surface textures.

The Challenges

However, acrylic paint dries quickly and the dried paint is not re-useable. This is perhaps acrylic's only disadvantage. It can be helpful on the other hand, because it allows you to over-paint without waiting long for an earlier layer of color to dry. It does make it more difficult to move paint around on the surface to blend colors. This merely requires better planning and a quicker work pace. It is a very good idea to have a shadow and light study sketch and a color scheme sketch prepared before working on the actual piece. You should try to leave as little paint on the palette as possible so you'll always have fresh paint. I usually use a flat porcelain dish as a palette. I tend to use an amount of paint that is only enough for one area or a "step" at a time – say up to 15 minutes before it gets dry, to prevent waste. I do not clean my palette regularly, rather I put new fresh paint on as needed. It is a good idea to keep paints moist while in use by spaying them with water from time to time. Covering the palette with plastic wrap will prevent paints from drying out while you are away from the painting.

Figure 8-1. *An acrylic color set. Photo by Wenhai Ma.*

The Palette

- Titanium White
- Lemon Yellow
- Cadmium Yellow
- Yellow Ocher
- Flesh Tone
- Orange
- Scarlet
- Magenta
- Violet
- Sepia
- Van Dyke Brown
- Cerulean Blue
- Prussian Blue
- Sap Green
- Viridian
- Green Deep
- Dark Grey
- Ivory Black

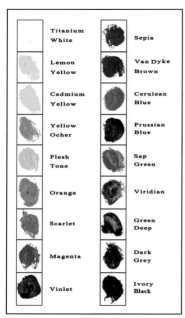

Titanium White	Sepia
Lemon Yellow	Van Dyke Brown
Cadmium Yellow	Cerulean Blue
Yellow Ocher	Prussian Blue
Flesh Tone	Sap Green
Orange	Viridian
Scarlet	Green Deep
Magenta	Dark Grey
Violet	Ivory Black

Figure 8-2. *A set of colors as shown in this chart should be sufficient for you to work on theatre renderings. Again, I would only squeeze out the paint I could use up in about 15 minutes on the palette.*

Get the "Greys" and Opaque Tones

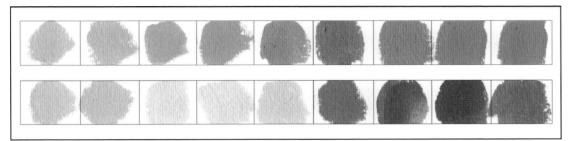

Figure 8-3. *The colors get opaque and pretty when white is added for various tones.*

Brushwork

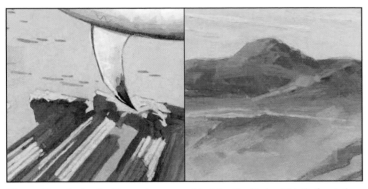

Figure 8-4. *Strokes should serve the purpose of depicting the objects – Note the fine strokes used to define the shark on the left, while the columns are depicted as a distant secondary layer. Note the subtle strokes used to build the mountains on the right.*

Using the Pigment as "Watercolor"

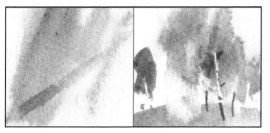
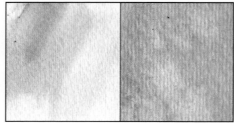

Figure 8-5. *These figures were done with the watercolor wet-in-wet and wet on dry techniques. I simply used acrylics in the same way I would watercolor.*

Figure 8-6. *You can create soft wash watercolor effects if the acrylic is used as watercolor without adding white.*

Using the Pigment as "Paint"

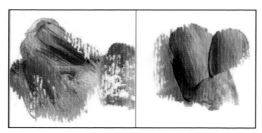

Figure 8-7. *Acrylics can be applied as thickly as if you were painting with oil. It creates exciting painterly effects.*

Working on Details and Fine Spots

Figure 8-8. *The details were obtained with fine-point round brushes.*

The Salt Texture Technique

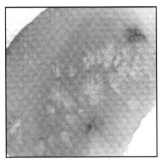

Figure 8-9. *You may also apply the salt texture technique as used in watercolor on acrylic washes. (See Chapter 7, pp. 133-134)*

Masking/Blocking Techniques

When you work on delicate details or straight lines, you might like to use some "tools" to help make the task easier. For example, when you want to paint an area and keep the edge straight and clean, you may use a piece of paper to block the side that you don't want to be painted, very similar to the pencil sketching techniques described in Chapter 4, *Preparing the Sketch*.

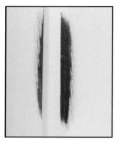

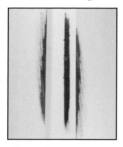

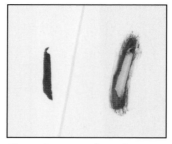

Figure 8-10. *A clean edge obtained by blocking the left side. You may find it helpful to use a soft flat brush and work carefully so that the paint does not go over the boundary.*

Figure 8-11. *A narrow line painted by blocking each side of the desired area with regular paper. Again, the use of a soft flat brush and a careful hand will prevent paint from spilling across the boundary.*

Figure 8-12. *A small area obtained by stenciling (cut-out stencil on the right). Again, you should use a soft flat brush.*

Workshop I

In this rendering for *Medea*, I wanted to show the strong contrast between blue and white to evoke the "Greek" impression, the blue ocean and the white architecture. The design was inspired by a sculpture by the Hillman Library in Pittsburgh that I walked by every day. Since the industrial-steel-like beams require good control over the straightness of lines, I used the blocking techniques quite a bit.

You will need:

Kitchen paper towel for cleaning your brush. It also helps you control the quantity of water in your brush.

Two containers with fresh water. You will always need to have a container of clean water in case you may need to wash away a stroke or an accident.

Many artists prefer to use acrylic on illustration board or mat board. For this rendering, however, I used watercolor paper.

Step 1

Figure 8-13. *A pencil sketch prepared on watercolor paper, 8½" x 11".*

Step 2

Figure 8-14. *I used Ivory Black and Prussian Blue to figure out the shadow and light effect. It should be noted that I did not use any white for this step. This step is very useful in obtaining a good idea of the lighting in the scene. I actually used my rough white card concept model, being lit by a desk light, as a reference.*

Step 3

Figure 8-15. *I applied some colors in places using the acrylic as if it were watercolor. I avoided the use of white for this step because I wanted to get a sense of the look of the rendering quickly but not actually build up the objects in color yet. Note that I used some Orange for the beams and Cerulean Blue for the CYC this time.*

Step 4

Figure 8-16. *I started to add white in Prussian Blue for the blue CYC to obtain an opaque effect, though I did not attempt to finish one area at a time. I applied some opaque paint on the shaded areas of the beams. I also applied some rough strokes on the stage floor. Note I did not bring the brightness to the final level yet.*

Step 5

Figure 8-17. *I worked on the CYC with more opaque and thick paint, on the beams and the stage floor. Because I did not wish to have to go back and work into this rendering any more after this stage, I worked on detailed individual areas very carefully. I wanted to keep the beams clean with a "solid" look so I used a piece of paper to block the side I did not want to paint and applied paint to the determined area as if I were using a stencil. Note that I used a fine-pointed round watercolor brush for the actors and the hanging hook-shaped "branches". I actually used a black ink pen and a ruler to reinforce the outlines of the "branches" before painting.*

Following are two more examples showing how renderings are done with acrylics. Because the steps are very similar to the rendering for *Medea* as shown in *Figure 8-15* through *8-17*, I will just skip the explanation but leave the sketches showing progression stages. Note the first figure is the shadow and light study sketch. See *Figures 8-18* to *22*.

Figures 8-18 through 8-22. A Street Scene, *rendering by Wenhai Ma. Acrylics on white mat board, 2009. 12" x 8 ¼".*

Figures 8-23 through 8-29. A Midsummer Night's Dream *under the Sea, a drop project as a demonstration for class by Wenhai Ma, 8½" x 11", 2009.* Figure 8-23 *is a Photoshop collage prepared as a color scheme study sketch.* Figure 8-24 *is a shadow and light study sketch, 8" x 11".*

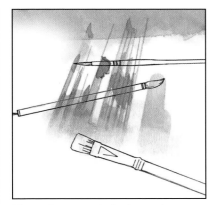

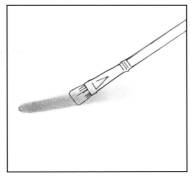

Figure 8-30. *Note the brushes I used are "Medium White Cloud", or watercolor round No. 8 for the large, bold strokes; watercolor round No. 2 for the fine lines and details. The No. 9 soft-hair flat brush was used for softening the bottom of the columns. I applied a few layers of white glaze, gradually blending them into the white background.*

Figures 8-31 and 8-32. *Note I used the same method working on the shark's belly. You may do some exercise as shown in* Figure 8-33, *simply using white to soften the end of a paint stroke.*

RENDERING WITH GOUACHE

"Real painters understand with a brush in their hand ... what does anyone do with rules? Nothing worthwhile."

Berthe Morisot (1841–1895)
French Impressionist painter.

Gouache has been used for a long time. It was primarily used for manuscripts. In the seventeenth century, it became more widely used as a painting medium by Italian and Dutch artists Zuccarelli and Van Dyck. Some of Toulouse Lautrec's (1864-1901) finest café scenes were painted with gouache on scraps of brown paper and cardboard. The color can be used thickly or it may be watered down to fine washes.

Gouache used to be a very popular media for scene design renderings in Russia and China. In Russia, especially in the late 19th century and first half of the 20th century, almost all the beautiful scene and costume renderings were done with gouache, or a combination with watercolor. It was also used widely for scenic painting in Europe, Russia, China and all over the world – though the pigment was not what we see in fine tubes and was not as expensive. The artists used to mix the pigment powder with glue, most often the smelly "rabbit skin glue."

In my times at the Central Academy of Drama in Beijing, all the scene designers, costume designers and lighting designer used gouache for their renderings. It is still a required medium for the competitive Entry Exams for admission to the Central Academy of Drama, the Central Academy of Fine Arts and lots of other art and design institutes in China. Such an exam usually requires the students to paint a set of still-life or a live model portrait on site within four hours.

The Challenges

Unlike oil, when you are done with your gouache rendering, you will find that values look different than they appeared when the paint was wet. Lighter tones generally dry slightly darker, while darker tones tend to dry slightly lighter. This makes it something of a challenge to match colors when that specific part is dry. However, unless you wish to re-work that area with new paint, you may carefully try to use a damp brush to rub off some paint nearby and use it to cover the needed spot. It also requires a good drawing foundation and comprehension of shadow and light. Your rendering can easily become opaque and muddy if white is improperly used.

Figure 9-1. En premiär (A premiere) *by Anders Leonard Zorn, 1888, gouache, 76cm x 56 cm.*

Figure 9-2. *Concept sketch by Wenhai Ma for* Summer and Smoke *by Tennessee Williams. Gouache over watercolor washes on illustration board, 11" x . 8½*

Figure 9-3. *Rendering by Wenhai Ma for* Marco Millions *by Eugene O'Neill, gouache on mat board, 20" x 16", 1984. This rendering shows the dry-brush technique I used for a decorative setting.*

Figure 9-4. *Gouache technique study after a Russian painting. Wenhai Ma, 1981.*

Figure 9-5. *Nude,* Wenhai Ma after a Russian oil painting. Gouache on paper, 30cm x 15cm, 1980.

The Paints

I usually use Winsor & Newton Gouache or Designer's Gouache. I've also found the Chinese brand Marie's works very well – probably because this pigment is very popular in China where gouache is still a favorite medium for theatre designers for their renderings and models and therefore the manufactures have really refined their product.

Gouache paints are sold in tubes, jars and bottles, often labeled as "designer's color." A vast range of colors is available. However, some of the bright fugitive colors are not recommended for fine permanent renderings.

Figure 9-6. *A set of gouache paint. Photo by Wenhai Ma*

Gouache paints are expensive in the States so my recommendation is that you invest your budget in only the most necessary colors, if not a set:

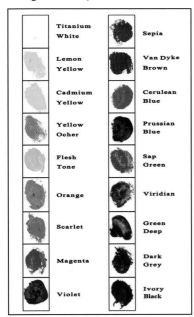

Figure 9-7. *A set of colors as shown in this chart should suffice for you to work on a theatre rendering.*

- Permanent White
- Lemon Yellow
- Yellow Ocher
- Orange
- Vermilion
- Scarlet
- Crimson Lake
- Violet
- Burnt Sienna
- Van Dyke Brown
- Ultramarine Blue
- Cobalt Blue
- Cerulean Blue
- Prussian Blue
- Green Deep
- Viridian
- Sap Green
- Lamp Black

I usually place the colors on my palette in the order as shown in the chart, either from White to Black, or from Black to White:

White is the most frequently used color. You may get a large jar or tube of white gouache for painting large areas in a hobby store at a lower price. The "washable poster paint" white is a reasonable alternative. However, for areas that require fine and detailed portrayal, you would be better served using professional Permanent White to get the best results.

Cheaper gouache colors are made opaque by the addition of white. Recall the cheap house paint we sometimes use for scenic painting – even the color "black" has white added in it! The best gouache is not manufactured by adding white but by using an extremely high level of pigmentation. This allows the artist to obtain any colors they want by using original, bright colors.

The artist gouache paint available at art supplies stores is a lot finer than scenic paint. It's bright, authentic in colors, convenient, flat and its re-useable nature makes it a favorite medium for theatre designers. It has a matte finish which can be very interesting in contrast to the semi-gloss finish obtained by acrylic. Because of this, it is an ideal pigment for model coloring, in combination with acrylics. My students love it for model coloring and paint elevations.

In the past, gouache was also called "watercolor" for it was a water-based pigment. The big difference between these two pigments is that watercolor is transparent and gouache is opaque.

The chart below shows colors mixed by water-based media. The upper row: watercolor – without white added for lighter hues; The lower row: gouache — with white added for lighter hues. As you can see, I tried to match the colors vertically to better illustrate the difference between the two media.

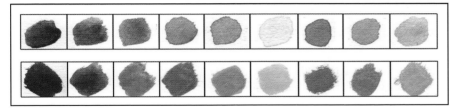

Figure 9-8. Upper row: watercolor; Lower row: gouache.

The Brushes

I use both flat brushes and round brushes for gouache rendering. Sable and artificial sable brushes work well. Large soft-hair brushes are good for bold brush strokes. New fine-pointed soft brushes are good for details. Old hard-hair brushes are good for dry brush techniques. There is also a brush with one hair only – perfect for those really fine details!

The Surface

I usually use watercolor paper 140lb or 300lb cold or hot press for my gouache renderings. Illustration board cold or hot press can be an ideal surface for gouache, too. I also find stretched canvases work very well for gouache. You may even ground the surface – either paper or canvas — with a thin layer of orange acrylic wash. Because acrylics are water resistant the wash cannot be picked up by your gouache once the acrylic wash dries.

Colored pastel paper gives you an interesting color base as you may occasionally leave certain spots uncovered and unpainted. I personally prefer warm grey-colored pastel paper to bright and strong colors.

Or, you may like have your watercolor paper tinted with a thin layer of watercolor first. Watercolor is easy to soak into watercolor paper and will not be picked up when you work on it later.

Figure 9-9. The brushes I usually use for my renderings with gouache. From top to bottom: No. 2 round, No. 8 round, ¾-inch flat, No. 6 flat and No. 4 flat.

The Stay-Wet Paint Container

It is a good idea to have your gouache paint stored in a stay-wet container. This kind of container allows you to keep paints squeezed out of the tubes into the cells. Every time after use, drop a couple of drops of clean water in each cell and cover the container with the lid. I also keep a piece of wet foam sponge inside my paint container. The colors remain damp and malleable while you are working and the lid keeps them still usable for up to a week or two after a working session. In case the paint gets dry, drop some clean water in each cell, and allow two hours for the paint to soak up the water before use. An eye dropper serves this purpose very well.

 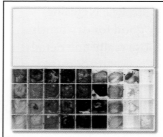

Figures 9-10 and 9-11. *The stay-wet paint container*

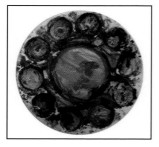

Figure 9-12. *This is a picture of the palette taken right after I finished the rendering for* The Storm *(Figures 9-17 through 9-23.) It may look boring and nasty but it worked well for my needs. Since I had a paint container, I simply used this palette as a surface for mixing colors. I tended not to leave much paint on it. I actually did not need to clean it up very often — the work is on the paper, not on the palette!*

Figure 9-13. *Rendering by Wenhai Ma for* Monkey King Wreaks Havoc in Heaven, *Peking Opera, gouache on mat board, 20" x 16", 1981. This rendering shows the dry-brush technique I used for a decorative, brightly-lit and colorful setting.*

Figure 9-14. *Rendering by Wenhai Ma for* The Way of the World *by William Congreve, gouache, colored pencils and watercolor on colored mat board, 1982. Note that I used thin, watered down gouache on the draperies, and applied dry strokes on the sky, the tiles on the floor, the actors, and the statue, and I used colored pencils for the highlights on the columns and the draperies.*

Figure 9-15. *A shadow and light study sketch by Wenhai Ma, gouache on paper, 1982.*

Figure 9-16. *Paint elevation by Wenhai Ma for a hanging panel for a Chinese Opera, the Hong Kong Academy for Performing Arts, gouache on mat board. The diamond shaped panel: 7" x 7", 2003.*

A plastic watercolor palette or a traditional oil pallet should work well for gouache. I sometimes just use a piece of plywood.

Workshop I

I will take my rendering for *The Storm* (by Alexander Ostrowski, Russian, 1823-1886) as an example to explain the progression. Gouache was not only a popular pigment for renderings but also the proper medium for this particular Russian play. It allowed me to represent my design with a painterly, oil-like style.

Step 1
I had the sketch well prepared on 140lb watercolor paper, taped onto a drawing board.

Figure 9-17. *Step 1.*

Step 2
I prepared a shadow and light study sketch. I shaded this one quickly with a No. 2 pencil on a photocopy. This step is necessary and highly recommended for it helps you remember the shadow and light and atmospheric quality on your rendering.

Figure 9-18. *Step 2.*

Step 3

I used dark brown, black and a touch of orange to work out shadow and light as if I was working with watercolor. No white was used for this step. Some spots of the colors in this step would be left as the final look.

Figure 9-19. *Step 3.*

Step 4

I had all the colors laid out quickly without fine details as if I was finishing the plate, though the colors will still need to be adjusted. This time, white is used for hues and tones. Note the paint I applied on paper was thicker and opaque but not chunky. I applied bold painterly strokes and deliberately left some spots showing the subtle watercolor-like base coat I did in *Figure 9-19*. I tried to make the colors as close to my original vision as possible.

Figure 9-20. *Step 4.*

Step 5

I adjusted the color and hue relations. Note I applied finer strokes on the background and lessened the contrast with the setting on the stage.

Figure 9-21. *Step 5.*

Step 6

I worked on the setting on the stage – the raked platform, the road, the benches and the shadows. Note I used the round #3 watercolor brush for the details such as the benches, the actor, the road and the seams of the wooden planks of the raked platform.

Figure 9-23. *This picture with the unfinished rendering was taken during the progression. You can see the paint, palette and brushes: a flat No. 3 flat brush and a No. 6 round watercolor brush.*

Figure 9-22. *Step 6. The finished rendering. 14" x 10.5", 2009.*

Below are three more examples showing how renderings are done with gouache. Because the steps are very similar to the rendering for *The Storm* as shown in *Figures 9-17 through 9-23*, I will just skip the explanation but leave the sketches showing progression stages. Note the tools I used for each step and various effects. This backdrop paint elevation was done on illustration board.

Workshop II

The Seascape

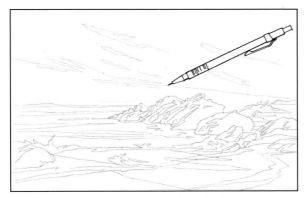

Figure 9-24. *Mechanical pencil, 0.3mm for the sketch.*

Figure 9-25. *3" soft hair flat brush for the washes.*

Figure 9-26. *No. 9 soft-hair flat brush for the blue ocean – horizontal strokes.*

Figure 9-27. *Soft-hair "Medium White Cloud" for the rocks. No. 8 round watercolor brush also works well.*

Figure 9-28. *No. 4 soft-hair flat brush for the highlights of the rocks.*

Figure 9-29. *No. 4 soft-hair flat brush and No. 2 round watercolor brush for the ocean foam, the fine highlights and for the clouds.*

Figure 9-30. *No. 4 soft-hair flat brush used for the beach and No. 2 round watercolor brush for the really fine lines representing the highlights on the surface of the water.*

Figure 9-31. *The finished rendering. Gouache on illustration board, 12 ½″ x 8 ¼″. 2009.*

I usually keep some of the first coat watercolor wash – without white added –as the finished transparent look. The thickness of the paint is dependent on the different effects desired. See *Figure 9-32* for detailed explanations.

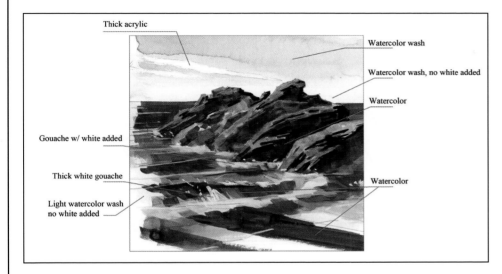

Figure 9-32. *A section of the Seascape by Wenhai Ma, 7¼" x 7¼", 2009.*

Workshop III

Winter in the Woods

Note the first figure is a reference photo and the second figure is a shadow and light study sketch.

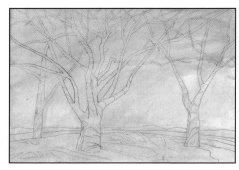

Figures 9-33 through 9-39. *Backdrop paint elevation:* Winter in the Woods *by Wenhai Ma. Gouache on illustration board. 11 ½″ x 8″, 2009.*

Workshop IV

The Banana Tree

Note the first figure is a reference photo I took and the second figure is the shadow and light study sketch.

Figures 9-40 through 9-42. *Paint elevation:* The Banana Tree. *Reference image, shadow and light study sketch and finished rendering for paint elevation. 6 ½" x 8", 2009.*

Figure 9-43. *The details showing the parts colored with watercolor and parts painted with thick gouache. 5 ½" x 4", 2010.*

Gouache w/ white added

Watercolor

Watercolor

Tranfered lines

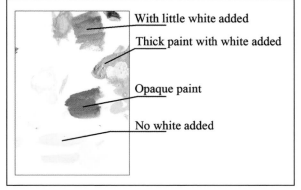

With little white added

Thick paint with white added

Opaque paint

No white added

Figure 9-44. *This chart shows various strokes and techniques applied on the Banana Tree.*

I usually use a fine-point brush with white gouache to pick up highlights on actors and scenic elements on some of my renderings. *See Figures 9-45 to 48.*

Figures 9-45 through 9-48. *Details of renderings by Wenhai Ma. From left to right and top to bottom:* The Hairy Ape *by Eugene O'Neill;* The Bald Soprano *by Eugène Ionesco;* Crazy Snow *The Shanghai Drama Art Center;* Duke Bluebeard's Castle *by Béla Bartók. Note how I highlighted the actors with gouache while the background was kept loose and relaxed.*

10

RENDERING WITH COLORED PENCILS

On the psychic effects of looking at color ...

"They produce a corresponding spiritual vibration, and it is only as a step towards this spiritual vibration that the elementary physical impression is of importance."

Wassily Wassilyevich Kandinsky (1866–1944)
Russian painter and art theorist.

DRAWING BY WENHAI MA

The Challenges

Though they may be considered the most "fearless" color media due to their highly controllable nature, it requires a good understanding of drawing and colors. The most challenging part is the shadow and light effect. It is always a good idea to have a shadow and light study sketch prepared with regular pencil before working with colors. The colored pencil lines are not fully erasable and thus, you need to be careful not to overwork on areas, particularly those that are supposed to be brightly lit. The other challenge for this particular scene is that the perspective can be quite tricky and complex. I worked on a piece of drafting paper, freehand to start with. I then used my ruler to check and finalize the lines. This step may take some time.

The Strokes & Blending

When drawing with colored pencil, there are a range of techniques which you can employ as with graphite pencil. The pencil stroke is a unique effect which other media do not possess. The strokes are pretty similar to the ones you get when you draw with regular pencils, especially when you hatch the strokes. Which one you choose will depends on the final effect you are aiming for. It is a good idea to spend some time exploring the colored pencil medium with small pieces before attempting a major drawing.

The chart below introduces some basic colored pencil strokes which will be useful in your drawing.

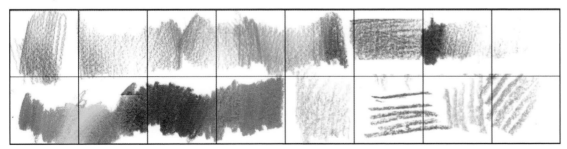

Figure 10-1. *Note how the pencil strokes are hatched, how the various colors and hues are progressed and how they are blended.*

It helps if you have a set of pencils with many colors to enable you to get the specific colors you want. However, it works very well if you work in the "Impressionistic" style – that is to mix colors by hatching the strokes, although the Impressionists hatched colors with brush dots and short brush strokes. It is also a helpful exercise to study how colors were hatched in the paintings of Impressionists such as Van Gogh or Pisarro by copying some masterpieces with colored pencils. *See Figure 10-4.*

Since it is very similar to the way you draw with graphite pencils, some drawing techniques can also be applied to colored pencil drawing.

Figure 10-2. The Sunset *by Wenhai Ma, oil pastels on paper,. 29" × 36¼", 1988.*

Figure 10-3. Entrance to the Village of Voisins *by Camille Pisarro (1830-1903), 36" x 29", oil on canvas, 1872, Musée d'Orsay, Paris, France. Reproduction by Shuqing Zhai, oil on canvas, 24" x 20", 1992.*

Figure 10-4. *Colored pencil sketch after Camille Pisarro's* Entrance to the Village of Voisins. *Wenhai Ma.*

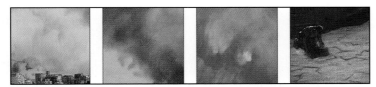

Figure 10-5 and 10-6. *Details of rendering for* Summer and Smoke *by Tennessee Williams, and details from other colored pencil renderings by Wenhai Ma.*

Note the background in *Figure 10-5* above, I hatched the pencil strokes very carefully and evenly. I then used a piece of tissue paper to rub the background so the colors were blended smoothly with a soft and subtle effect.

Workshop I

Orpheus Descending

You will need a set of colored pencils.

Step 1
I took my time figuring out the sketch with correct perspective and had it scanned, printed on paper, 90 lb, 8 ½" x 11". Note I also adjusted the color to make the line appear as sepia tone.

Figure 10-7. *Step 1.*

Step 2

I tinted the sketch with a light orange watercolor wash and intended to keep some of it eventually. Note that I left the center area a little bit lighter to suggest the lighting effect.

Figure 10-8. *Step 2.*

Step 3

I shaded the sketch as if it was a pencil shadow and light study sketch. Pencils used: Dark Blue and Dark Brown.

Figure 10-9. *Step 3.*

Step 4

I added more colors: Dark Blue for the exterior, the surroundings and some shadows. Yellow Light for the light hanging from the ceiling.

Figure 10-10. *Step 4.*

Step 5

I added more colors: Red, Orange, Red Umber, depicting all the details and worked on certain areas in depth. Note that I used a No. 2 round watercolor brush and with white gouache picked up some of the highlights. In *Figure 10-10*, I drew some details separately: the dresses and hats and some signs for various departments of the dry goods store in the scene. I intended to put them on the downstage left wall using Photoshop.

Figures 10-11 and 10-12. *Step 5.*

Step 6

Sketch by Wenhai Ma for *Orpheus Descending*, by Tennessee Williams, Duke University, colored pencils over ink sketch on drawing paper, 9 ½" x 6 ½", 2009.

I sometimes also use white colored pencil to pick up highlights. See *Figure 10-14*.

Figure 10-13. *Finished sketch, 11" x 8 ½", 2010.*

Figure 10-14. *Details of rendering by Wenhai Ma for Electra in* The Greeks *directed by Mel Shapiro, 1983. Note how I highlighted the texture of the wrinkled plastic by using a white pencil.*

11

RENDERING WITH WATER-SOLUBLE PENCILS

"Drawing and color are not separate at all; insofar as you paint, you draw. The more the color harmonizes, the more exact the drawing becomes."

Paul Cézanne (1839–1906)
French artist and Post-Impressionist painter.

DRAWING BY WENHAI MA

The Challenges

Though the "drawing" stages may be less nerve-wracking they still require a solid understanding of color and a firm grasp of drawing technique. The water washing phases can also be tricky. It helps if you have done some watercolor practice prior to working with water-soluble pencils.

The Strokes

The pencil strokes are pretty much like those used when you draw with regular pencils, especially the way to hatch the strokes.

Get the Colors

It helps if you have a set of pencils with ample colors to allow you to attain the specific colors you want. However, it works very well if you work in the "Impressionistic" way – to "weave", or hatch colors, though the Impressionists "wove" colors with brush dots and short brush strokes. I find it quite interesting to have a cool color with a warm color hatched over it.

Blending

I tend not to blend the colors because I appreciate the quality that pencil strokes give the rendering. You may use a piece of tissue paper to smudge if desired, but remember you will wash the sketch with brushes in later phases and so you might not need to worry about blending colors.

Washing

A soft-hair 2" flat brush and a No. 8 soft-hair round watercolor brush both work very well for the washing. I tend not to wash too much so some of the pencil strokes remain. In fact, the colors may get dull and muddy if you over-wash an area. When I work on details or small areas, I use a smaller soft-hair round watercolor brush with some extra attention. I do mainly "atmospheric" and "impressionist" type of renderings with water-soluble pencils so I usually do not worry about portraying fine details anyway. The line sketch plays an important part in

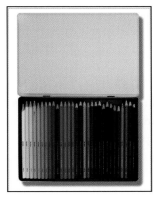

Figure 11-1. *A set of water-soluble pencils, or watercolor pencils.*

stating the fine details. When needed, I may simply use a fine-pointed brush and watercolor instead to get the details. I usually do not use the white water-soluble pencil, the same as in watercolor.

Masking/Blocking Techniques

Since the "drawing" phases are very similar to how you use regular drawing pencils, the same drawing techniques can also be applied to the water-soluble pencils. That is, you may use a piece of paper to block an area so you will keep your strokes within the boundary, and to portray a small spot by using a stencil or paper cut-out.

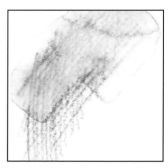

Figure 11-2. *The pencil strokes are dissolved by the wet brush. It is quite a unique effect! Illustration by Wenhai Ma.*

WORKSHOP I

This is a backdrop I designed for the ballet *The Unicorn, the Gorgon, the Manticore* for Duke University Dance Program in 1988. The design was inspired by some of William Turner's artworks. Since I wanted to keep the painterly strokes and the watercolor effect, I found that the water-soluble pencils were the perfect media. The drop was painted on gauze with transparent colors.

Tools

I used the Swiss-made Caran d'Ache brand pencils for this project. You may of course use an alternative brand of high quality. I also used two brushes with soft bristles: the 3" FLT SHT HN flat bush and the round "Medium White Cloud" brush. I worked on a sheet of Strathmore cold press watercolor paper, 140 lb, sized 9" x 12".

Figure 11-3. *The pencils and brushes I used for this particular rendering. Photo by Wenhai Ma.*

Step 1
I outlined the design lightly with a No. 2 pencil.

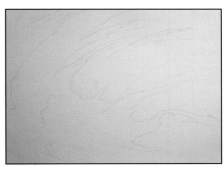

Figure 11-4. *Step 1.*

Step 2
I started using a blue pencil, applying some pencil strokes.

Figure 11-5. *Step 2.*

Step 3
I applied some orange pencil strokes.

Figure 11-6. *Step 3.*

Step 4

I applied more pencils strokes with more colors such as red, flesh tone, yellow, purple and brown.

Figure 11-7. *Step 4.*

Step 5

I used my 3" flat brush and carefully washed over the pencil strokes from the light areas to the dark areas to avoid darkening the focus point and so the light contrast was well-kept.

Figures 11-8 and 11-9. *Step 5.*

Step 6

I reinforced certain areas by applying more pencil strokes and washed over them carefully with my round "Medium White Cloud" brush. Note that I hatched the pencil strokes as I described in the beginning of the chapter.

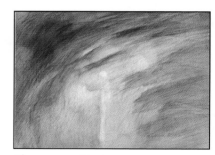

Figure 11-10. *Step 6.*

Step 7

I framed the drop with the proscenium and masking on the stage. I included some dancers, too. The dancers were drawn with pencil and colored with water-soluble pencils. I then put it all together with Photoshop. The floor was quoted from the drop but edited with Photoshop.

Below are more examples showing how rendering is done with water-soluble pencils. Because the steps are very similar to the rendering for *The Unicorn, the Gorgon, the Manticore* as shown in *Figures 11-4 through 11-11*, I will just skip the explanation but leave the sketches showing progression stages. Note that since that drop was designed as a transparency, I did not use any white but left the paper itself as white. The line sketch was done with an H pencil.

Figure 11-11. *Step 7.*

Note the tools I used for each step and various effects. This backdrop paint elevation was done on cold press watercolor paper, 140 lb. I stretched the paper on the drawing board using trimmed paper strips and white glue, instead of tape. The surface was extremely taut which really allows for the pencil and brush strokes to go down smoothly. See Chapter 4: *Preparing the Sketch*, Stretching the Paper, *Figures 4-41 through 4-45* for reference. That lesson demonstrates stretching the paper with gummed tape. However you can follow the exact same steps but substitute the gummed tape for paper strips with white glue applied with a flat brush instead.

WORKSHOP II

The Castle

Note the second figure is a shadow and light study sketch, sized 8 ½" x 11". *See Figures 11-12 through 19* below.

Figures 11-12 through 11-18 . *Rendering by Wenhai Ma, 15 ½" x 10", 2009.*

Figures 11-19. *Rendering by Wenhai Ma, 15 ½″ x 10″, 2009.*

12

ACTORS/CHARACTERS IN RENDERINGS

"All the world's a stage
And all the men and women merely players:
They have their exits and their entrances;
And one man in his time plays many parts,
His acts being seven ages."
                (from As You Like It, *Act II, Scene VII)*

William Shakespeare (1564–1616)
English poet and playwright.

DRAWING BY WENHAI MA

A set usually does not live without actors and actions in it. The actors or characters play a big role in the completion of the design and "picturization." In a theatre design rendering, it is necessary to include actors/characters, so we may tell the proportions and their relationship to the sets as we see in models. It is even better if the characters in the scene are in the right costumes representing the dramatic action and the energy for a specific moment.

You may "import" figures from magazines, costume history books or existing production photographs. I usually create my own actors for my renderings. I enjoy posing the characters and taking snapshots with a digital camera on a tripod, based on the scene and action I imagine. I then add the poses to my rendering and add proper costumes so they become characters!

Figures, actors or characters in scene renderings require simplified, theatrical aspects. Besides, a good comprehension of the script and dramatic movement, tension and "picturization" really helps. Though I am by no means a director, I enjoy observing how directors work with stage movement, blocking and picturing actors with the setting on the stage. The directing class I took at Carnegie Mellon years ago really helped me understand these principles.

Figure drawing requires a good understanding of the human anatomy and movement. When I was a student at the Central Academy of Drama in Beijing, I was in the drawing studio every morning, most of the time working with live models. However, young scene designers seem to be kept a lot busier with other responsibilities and find themselves with no time to draw. This is sad because limited drawing skills may limit your working abilities and efficiency, plus the quality of your creativity and artistry.

I therefore strongly encourage young designers to find time to take figure drawing classes and keep drawing all the time. Even when you are too busy to draw actual life models you may copy figures from master figure drawings, good illustrations, good costume renderings, magazines, etc. Anything helps. It trains your eyes and hand and helps you understand figures and figures in movement.

Though there are no short cuts in figure drawing, I want to show you ways to create "simplified" figures in your renderings.

The Proportion of Human Figures

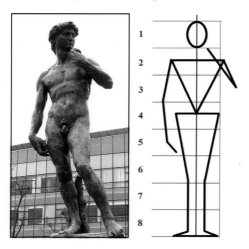

Figure 12-1. *Accurate 8-head-high adult male human figure. Left: Bronze reproduction of David by Michelangelo, in front of the Ningbo Grand Theatre, gifted by the Florence government, sister city of Ningbo, China. Photo and sketch by Wenhai Ma.*

Study from a Mannequin

Besides the exercises in the figure drawing classroom, it also helps to use a wooden mannequin as a "model", or rather a reference, to develop figures and poses. See *Figure 12-2*. Though the figures were from the mannequin, I added some flare from my own imagination.

Develop a Figure with Costume from a Mannequin

Drawings below show figures in movement and poses, with costumes developed from a mannequin.

Figure 12-2.

Figure 12-3. *The Little Men, 3-D animation figures and pencil figures by Richard Van As. Maya and pencil on paper, 2010. This is a fine example of the dramatic movement created by computer and how it may be developed into costumed figures. Courtesy of the artist.*

Figures 12-4 through 12-8. *Note that though I took the mannequin poses as references, I added lots of my own observation on the characters and made them "alive."*

When you do not have a model, or even a mannequin to draw from, you may simply grab an art book and copy the figures as if you drew from life. See *Figures 12-9 and 12-10.*

Figures 12-9 and 12-10. *Drawings from the sketch book, Wenhai Ma, 1993.*

Keep Drawing

You may also want to learn to draw faces in a few strokes, capturing the characteristics and features quickly – almost as if you are working on caricature drawings. See *Figures 12-11 and 12-12.*

Figures 12- 11 and 12-12. *Sketches by Wenhai Ma, 1993.*

Figure 12-13. *Faces from illustrations by Wenhai Ma. Watercolor and India ink.*

Hands Developed from a Mannequin

Though a mannequin hand is limited in movement, it may still be a good tool to learn the basic proportion of the parts, the fingers. See *Figures 12-14 and 12-15*.

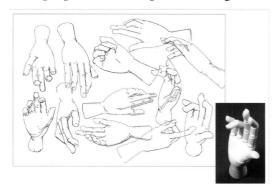

Figure 12-14. *Hands developed from a mannequin. Photoshop sketch by Wenhai Ma.*

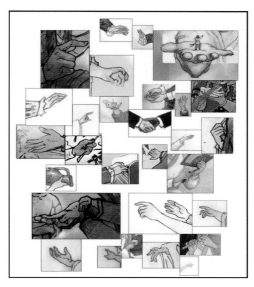

Figure 12-15. *Hands from illustrations by Wenhai Ma. Watercolor and India ink.*

Life Figure Drawing

Since there are no short-cuts in figure drawing, it is extremely helpful, even integral to do some actual life drawing exercises. Working on mannequins alone will not work. The best and most direct way to improve your drawing skills is simply the old way with the old medium: Draw with a pencil. See *Figures 12-16 through 12-26*.

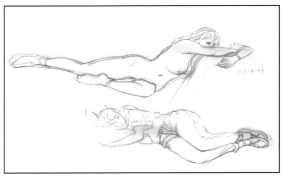

Figures 12-16 through 12-20. *Drawings by Wenhai Ma. Pencil on drawing paper and sketch pad.*

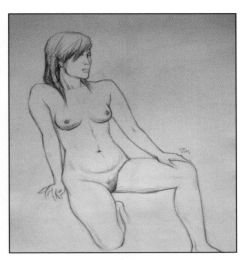

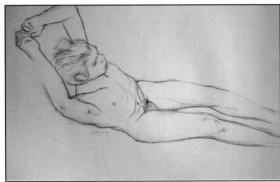
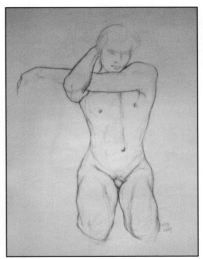

Figures 12-21 through 12-26. *Drawings by Wenhai Ma. Pencil on drawing paper and sketch pad.*

Draw with Pastels

There are two popular types of pastels: soft pastels and oil pastels, and both are good for figure drawing. Colored pastel paper works very well for both soft and oil pastels. See *Figures 12-27 through 12-30.*

Figures 12-28 and 12-29. *Drawings by Wenhai Ma. Soft pastels on paper, 2004.*

Figure 12-27. *Drawing by Yaoyao Ma Van As. Soft pastels on paper, 2005.*

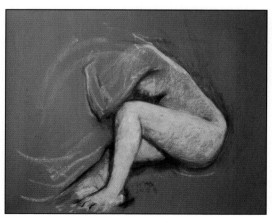

Figure 12-30. *Drawing by Wenhai Ma. Oil pastels on paper, 2004.*

The figures below are illustration by Wenhai Ma for various picture books. Note the poses for the characters were mainly poses by life models. They properly show the theatrical aspects and dramatic quality.

Develop a Character from a Model

Figures 12-31 and 12-32. *Illustrations and photos by Wenhai Ma.*

Figures 12-33 through 12-36. *Illustrations and photos by Wenhai Ma.*

Composition and Theatrical Grouping

French artist Jean-Baptiste-Siméon Chardin (1699 - 1779) painted a good number of still-life paintings. These still-life paintings show carefully balanced composition, carefully selected objects of various textures and soft diffusion of light. Even the compositions in his artworks alone can be of value for us to study. See *Figures 12-37 through 12-42*.

Figure 12-37. Autumn *by Shuqing Zhai, oil on board. 14" x 12". Note the reflection on top of the table.*

Figure 12-38. Still-life *by Shuqing Zhai, Oil on canvas, 35½" x 23 ½", 1992.*

Figure 12-39. Still-life *by Shuqing Zhai, Oil on canvas, 33 x 41, 1994.*

Figure 12-40. *Illustration by Wenhai Ma for* The Sun Catcher, *watercolor and India ink on paper. Note how the figures are grouped while each has its own characteristics and pose. This is something like what we call "picturization" on the stage.*

Figure 12-41. A View from the Monastery, *by Wenhai Ma. Oil on canvas, 32" x 24", 2006. Note how the six monks are grouped harmoniously, and yet each has a unique pose. Also note the way they are spaced.*

Figure 12-42. *Detail view from illustration for the* Making of Monkey King, *Pan Asian Publications, (USA) Inc. Watercolor and India ink, 1997. Note how the eighty or so figures are grouped. The focal point was emphasized in several ways: through the spacing, the use of color and light contrast.*

Figure 12-43. *Cropped renderings showing actors in various scenes. All by Wenhai Ma.*

In my theatre design renderings, I usually include my own interpretation of how my design is utilized and functions with actors.

The figures below show how I posed for all the actors in the "play within the play" scene for *Hamlet* and the scene when Petruchio rides in on horseback for the wedding in *The Taming of the Shrew*. I usually use a digital camera with a tripod to take pictures like these. I edit the figures and group them, and paste them into my sketch with Photoshop. I then have this sketch printed, use tracing paper to work on top of it. The costumes are created by my own perception.

Figures 12-44 and 12-45. *In the figure on the left, the figures photographed are larger in scale – it just made them easier to check. However, I edited them with Photoshop into the right proportion, in perspective.*

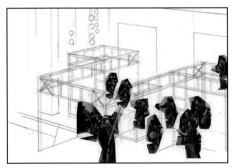 

Figures 12-46 and 12-47. *I found it was particularly necessary to include actors in the rendering so I could show how they were related within the environment.*

13

MIXED MEDIA AND
COMPUTER AIDED RENDERING

"The hand is the tool of tools."

Aristotle (384 BC–322 BC)
Greek philosopher and polymath.

DRAWING BY WENHAI MA

More than One Medium

Many times, I use more than one medium for my renderings. I usually start with watercolor on a pencil or ink sketch and highlight certain spots with gouache. In addition, I sometimes use a white colored pencil or a China marker for certain lines and sometimes on top of all that I might use water-soluble pencils for some added texture and sketchy effect.

To use these media to their fullest potential, you need to know their natural capacity and characteristics. There are advantages and disadvantages for each medium. The trick is to take those weaknesses and turn them into strengths. For example, the disadvantage for watercolor is that it is so tricky to control and you often get "accidents." However if you know this medium well, things can be controlled and these spontaneous accidents may turn out to be of benefit after all. It is the same for acrylics. The disadvantage for acrylics is that the paint dries too fast. While this is true, it also allows you to put down layers and glazes quickly. As stated in Chapter 5, *Pigments & Media*, each medium has its own strength and unique attributes.

Below is a summary of quick hints and tips for some of the more commonly used rendering media. You have to know them well to use them well!

Watercolor: Transparent, good for the background, great at creating an atmospheric base and it is also good for creating lighting effects.

Gouache: Opaque, rich in color, good for painterly renderings, paint elevation, model coloring, small spots over watercolor such as stars, lights, snowflakes and lightning.

Colored pencils: Semi-opaque and easily guided by a ruler. I occasionally use a white colored pencil to pick up some lines.

Acrylic: Can be applied as opaque or transparent, is water resistant, rich and bright in color, dries fast. It has a glossy finish when it dries.

Markers: Transparent and bright in color. While possessing some of the feel of watercolor, they are easy to control. They can work well over watercolor groundings and over ink line sketches. They feature interesting solid, firm strokes.

Oil: Opaque or transparent, water resistant and dries very slowly. The colors can be bright, rich and stay the same after they dry. It is good for paint elevations with a painterly approach. Since it dries so slowly, it allows for great blending of colors.

The computer can also be called a "medium". It does have its own unique advantages. Computers may undertake certain tasks and obtain certain effects that no traditional media can do. Computer technology makes certain tasks a great deal easier and more effective. Thus, computers should be regarded as nothing more than a helpful tool and therefore, can work with or enhance traditional media very well.

Computer-Aided Rendering

I have found that Photoshop is a very helpful tool for theatre designers. However, your computer is nothing magical and there isn't such a thing as getting it done by "touching a button". It is a tool, a pencil, a brush, a ruler, like what we use traditionally. Just like what we normally do, without "mind and hands" you cannot create good drawings even if you have the best pencil and brush. You will also need to have a good comprehension and sense of the design elements: line, shape, form, space, texture, value, colors, shadow and light, etc.

I have seen well-done computer-aided renderings and they are truly beautiful. I have also seen unsophisticated computer-aided renderings and they turn out to be mechanical, graphic and boring. I believe that those renderings were done with very limited sense and attention to the design elements.

When a line sketch is scanned, a great option nowadays is to color it with Photoshop.

Besides knowing the computer program tools and commands, you will need to "hand draw" and "hand render" well. This helps you to render with a different tool – the computer. You are dealing with the same elements as the traditional ones – line, shape, form, space, texture, value, colors, perspective and shadow and light.

You may need to collect lots of images for a single computer-aided rendering. Your rendering will include the theatre "house", may include a hardwood floor, wall with wallpaper, furniture, windows, doors, staircase, back drop, masking, actors in costumes, set dressing items, and a lot more. It is by no means easier or some kind of a magic way to render. However, as you practice, you will master skills and work more efficiently.

After opening the scanned line sketch in Photoshop, you may use Brush #14 to "wash" the sketch with various opacity and flow, as you do on actual watercolor paper. The Brush #14 stroke imitates actual brushwork quite well. In fact, since you may always backspace (delete and "redo") the steps, there is no need to worry about making mistakes.

You may like to get color variations – play with the warm and cool colors, as you do on actual watercolor paper. You may also have some color wash strokes prepared on watercolor paper; you can then import and paste them onto your Photoshop rendering. This may add some interesting atmospheric watercolor or painterly effect – to avoid "product design" or a cartoon look.

You may also try to work this way: Have the line sketch prepared on watercolor paper. Apply some "atmospheric" washes on it as you normally do. Have it scanned and opened in Photoshop, then color the rest from there. You may paint or patch textures, patch certain details from the paint elevations, adjust colors and brightness and contrast, transform scales, rotate, etc. You may also import actors from the costume renderings, furniture, etc. Eventually, when most of the scenic elements are settled, apply mist and fog effect, lighting effect, etc., as it may require.

Here are some Photoshop-aided renderings I did with notes below explaining some of the "tricks" involved.

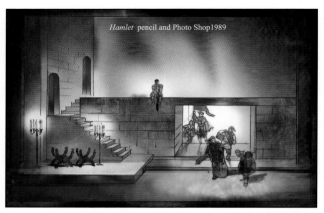

Figure 13-1. *Photoshop colored rendering over a hand drawn sketch by Wenhai Ma for* Hamlet *by William Shakespeare, 2008.*

Figure 13-2. *This thumbnail sketch was done very quickly. It was meant to have the idea of the composition drawn roughly. 3″ x 2 ½″, pencil.*

Figure 13-3. *This sketch was printed on watercolor paper, cold press, 90 lb. The lines are sepia, adjusted with Photoshop.*

Figure 13-4. *I applied some basic "atmospheric" watercolor strokes, wet-in-wet. I colored the actors also with watercolor,.10″ x 7 ½″.*

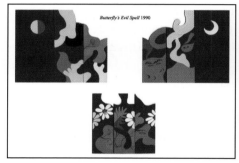

Figure 13-5. *Paint elevations. Gouache on mat board.*

Figure 13-6. *I patched the paint elevations onto the scenic elements. I patched in the backdrop (edited from the paint elevations). I created the lighting effect and the mist by using the eraser tool. I also did the masking. All of these were done with Photoshop. Rendering by Wenhai Ma for* Butterfly's Evil Spell *by Garcia Lorca, Duke University. Watercolor, gouache and Photoshop, 2009.*

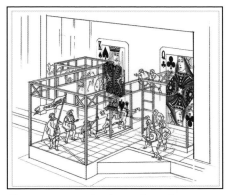

Figure 13-7. *Note that the K and Q cards were patched in. The Skew tool helped with the perspective.*

The following five figures show how the Photoshop-aided rendering for *The Trojan Women* was created. The design was for a black box with two sides of audience in a tennis court seating configuration.

Figure 13-8. *I started with a very small pencil sketch to explore the lighting effect – it is sized 3" x 1 ¼" - almost a "thumbnail" literally. Pencil on paper.*

Figure 13-9. *Sketch printed on watercolor paper, 140lb, 12 ¾" x 6 ½". The sepia color was adjusted with Photoshop.*

Figure 13-10. *Note I applied brush strokes mainly with Vandyke Brown for the overall picture and a couple of strokes with Prussian Blue in contrast with the brown. Occasionally I applied mid-tones mixed using brown and blue. Note I kept a strong contrast.*

Figure 13-11. *These are the paint elevations I made for each end of the "tennis court". Watercolor, water-soluble pencils and gouache on light grey mat board, 8" x 6" each, 1991.*

Figure 13-12. *Note the paint elevations were inserted with Photoshop. I used the Skew tool to adjust the perspective, locating them within the frames in perspective. Rendering by Wenhai Ma, 2009.*

The following five figures show how the Photoshop-aided rendering for *Full Moon* was created. The design was for a proscenium stage with a thrust apron.

Figure 13-13. *Pencil sketch on drawing paper, 8 ½" x 11".*

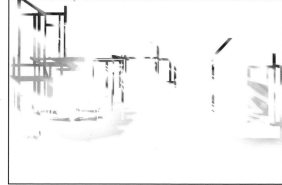

Figure 13-14. *Photoshop colored the skeleton of the houses. I kept this as a separated layer because it was convenient for me to adjust the brightness and color.*

Figure 13-15. *Photoshop color "washes." I applied patches of colors and textures with the edges softened by using the eraser tool. Note the foliage was cropped from an oil landscape I painted before. I patched a portion into the cheesecloth hanging above. The shadows on the floor were created with various tools such as the Paint Brush tool and the Polygonal Lasso tool. Note I paid attention to the lighting effect and kept the contrast very strong.*

Figure 13-16. *This is the layer with most of the colors and without the line sketch. I took my time working on the details, balancing the color and light.*

Figure 13-17 . *Finished rendering by Wenhai Ma for* **Full Moon**, *by Reynolds Price, Duke University, 1987.*

For small sized renderings, you may take advantage of the computer and have your pencil sketches scanned, adjusted and printed on watercolor paper.

Figure 13-18. *Rendering by Wenhai Ma for* Watership Down, *original novel by Richard Adams. Adapted by John Hildreth, directed by Katie McLean Hainsworth, Lifeline Theatre, Chicago, 2011. Photoshop over scanned pencil sketch and watercolor texture.*

Figure 13-19. *Photoshop collage for a scene design concept sketch for* Summer and Smoke, *by Tennessee Williams.*

THE STORYBOARD

"Put life into the imagined circumstances and actions until you have completely satisfied your sense of truth and until you have awakened a sense of faith in the reality of your own sensations."

Constantin Sergeyevich Stanislavski (1863–1938)
Russian actor and theatre director.

Storyboarding originated in the film industry and animation industry but I find it also very useful in theatre design. A storyboard is helpful for communication amongst the production team members, especially for musicals and large scaled productions that involve lots of scene changes and scene shifting. Once I designed a musical set which had over fifty scene changes. It was even difficult for me, the designer to remember all the scene changes and the sequence. The storyboard I created really helped me and everyone else in the team. The stage manager particularly loved it!

I usually have a sheet of mat board with the elevation sketches pasted on the left side and the ground plans pasted on the right side so it is convenient to tell how the turntable revolves, how the platforms shift, how the show curtain is dropped and how the furniture is moved around.

Each thumbnail need not be large. The ones I have done are about 2.5" x 3.5" in size. The ground plan should be about the same size so the two can be read as information in a pair easily. I sometimes even include the intermission with the house curtain dropped down so I may have a clear visual record of what's going on on the stage. I also put a short note below each sketch indicating the Act, Scene, the location, maybe also how the scene is shifted.

It may make the work more efficient if you start with a major scene with most of the scenic elements on the stage. This sketch can be a pencil perspective sketch of the usual size – around 8 ½" x 11". Then, you may reduce it on a photocopier to the desired size.

Make copies, as many as needed for all the scene changes. Change each scene. You may use whiteout to cover the parts that are shifted or removed and pencil in the new elements. Or, you may literally cut and shift an element by using a pair of scissors. Of course you may add actors in each scene.

When the line sketches are done, make a photocopy of each. Then you may color on the clean copy quickly with water-soluble pencils or simple watercolor washes. Because the thumbnails do not requires details, regular copy paper is OK for the simple coloring. See *Figures 14-1 and 14-2* below.

Figures 14-1 and 14-2. *Thumbnails done with water-soluble pencils over line sketches. All by Wenhai Ma. Approximately 2.5" x 3.5".*

You can then do the same for the thumbnail ground plans, except they need not be colored.

Next, trim these thumbnails and put them together on a sheet of mat board or card stock in the correct sequence, with the ground plan for each scene beside its counterpart. I usually place them to the right.

The figures below show some storyboards for various productions I have done.

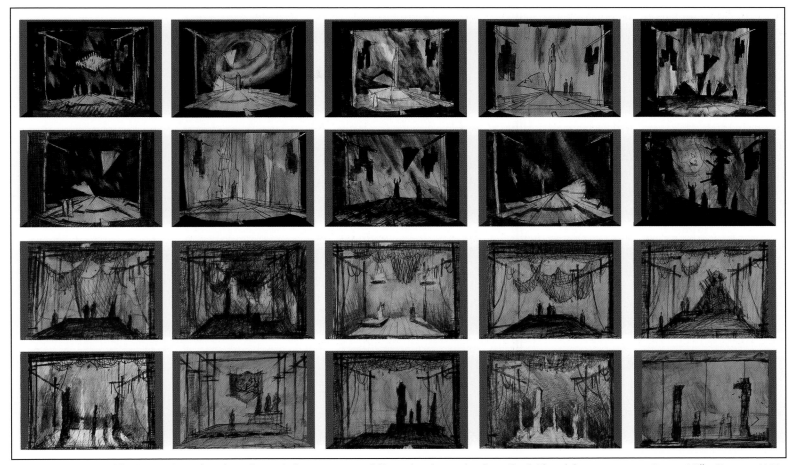

Figure 14-3. *Storyboard for* The Greeks*, set design by Wenhai Ma, ball-point pen, water-soluble pencils and watercolor, 5" x 3 ½" each. The early brain-storm version. Carnegie Mellon University, 1984.*

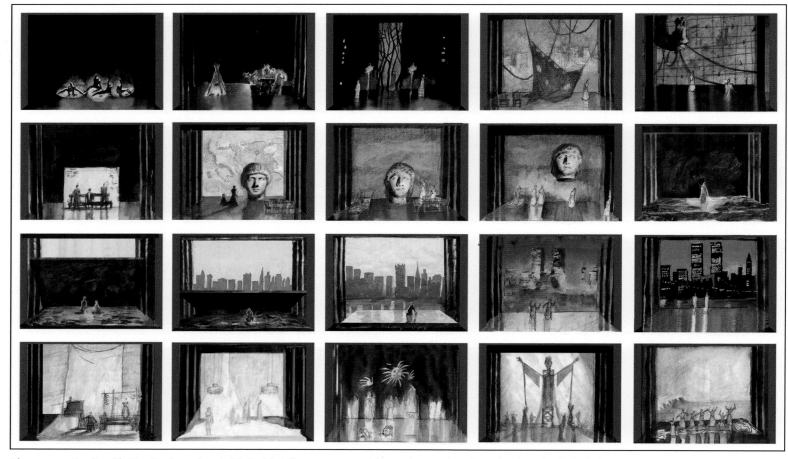

Figure 14-4. *Storyboard for* The Greeks, *set design by Wenhai Ma, ball-point pen, water-soluble pencils, watercolor and gouache, 5" x3 ½" each, The final version. Carnegie Mellon University, 1984.*

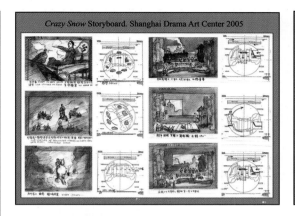

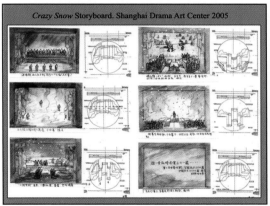

Figures 14-5 through 14-9. *Storyboard by Wenhai Ma for* Crazy Snow, *a musical premiered by the Shanghai Dramatic Center, 2005. Water-soluble pencils, watercolor, gouache over photocopies, 3″x2 ½″ each.*

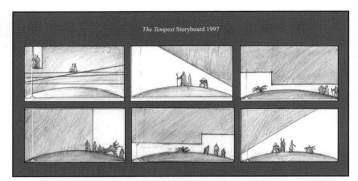

The Tempest Storyboard 1997

Figure 14-10. *Storyboard by Wenhai Ma for* The Tempest *by William Shakespeare, 1996, pencil on paper 3" x2.5".*

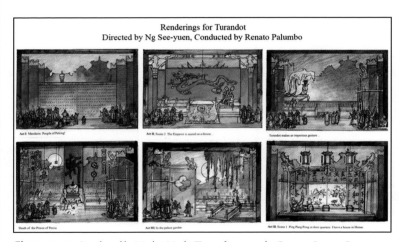

Renderings for Turandot
Directed by Ng See-yuen, Conducted by Renato Palumbo

Figure 14-11. *Storyboard by Wenhai Ma for* Turandot, *music by Giacomo Puccini. Stage director: Woo Seeyuen; Conductor: Renato Palumbo. Hong Kong Opera Company, Ltd., 2005, watercolor, water-soluble pencils on reduced photocopies, 6 ¼" x 4 ¼" each.*

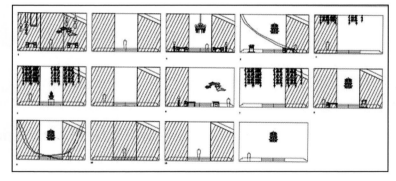

Figure 14-12. *Storyboard by Wenhai Ma for* Lost in Balcony Fog, *Kunjun Opera, 2008, AutoCAD.*

GALLERY

"True artists are almost the only men who do their work for pleasure."

François-Auguste-René Rodin (1840–1917)
French sculptor.

DRAWING BY WENHAI MA

In the years gone by, I have produced a vast number of scene and costume renderings for class projects, realized productions and classes I have taught. Watercolor, gouache, colored pencils, and watercolor pencils have been my media of choice. Occasionally, I use oil for certain effects that cannot be obtained by using other media. I also use the computer as a tool to render.

In this gallery chapter, I've put together a collection of some of my own scene and costume renderings. I have proudly included some of my students' work, with their permission, of course. I hope that these renderings are a valuable source of reference for our young designers in their study and professional development.

Figures 15-1 through 15-6. *Renderings by Wenhai Ma for* The Storm, *by Alexander Ostrowski (1823-1886, Russian), 12" x 9.5", 1981,*

Figures 15-7 through 15-11. *Renderings by Wenhai Ma for* The Hairy Ape *by Eugene O'Neill, watercolor, white gouache and white pencil on illustration board, 8 ½" x 11", 1982.*

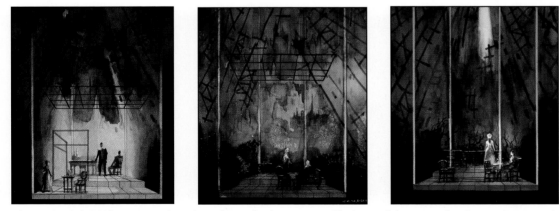

Figures 15-12 through 15-14. *Renderings by Wenhai Ma for* The Master Builder *by Henrik Ibsen, watercolor, white gouache over pencil sketch on illustration board, 5 ½" x 8 ½". Note the salt effect on the background.*

Figures 15-15 through 15-17. *Renderings by Wenhai Ma for* The Way of the World, *by William Congreve, 1982, 12″ x 9″, watercolor, gouache, colored pencils on tinted illustration board.*

Figure 15-18. *Rendering by Wenhai Ma for* Hamlet, *by William Shakespeare, 1982, 9″ x 7.5″, charcoal pencil on tinted mat board.*

Figures 15-19 through 15-22. *Renderings by Wenhai Ma for* Duke Bluebeard's Castle, *watercolor, gouache on illustration board. 1982.*

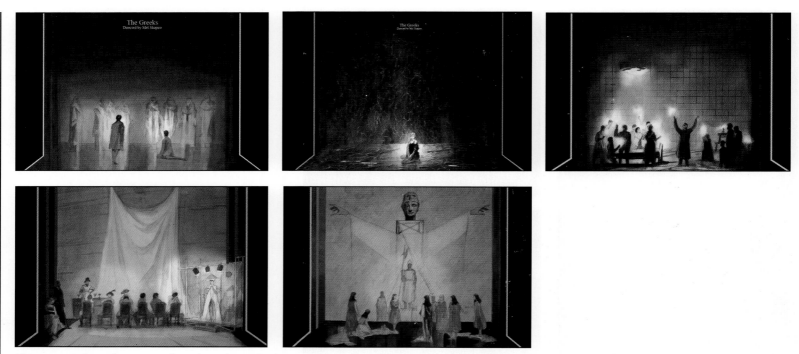

Figures 15-23 through 15-27. *Renderings by Wenhai Ma for* The Greeks, *directed by Mel Shapiro, 1983, watercolor, gouache, water-soluble pencils on illustration board. 9″ x 12″.*

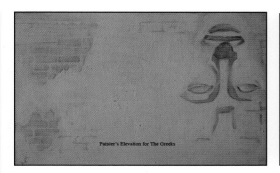

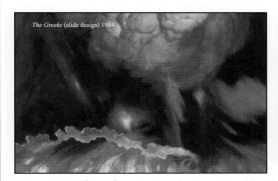

Figures 15-28 through 15-31. *Paint elevations prepared for slide projection by Wenhai Ma for* The Greeks, *directed by Mel Shapiro, 1983, pencil, watercolor, gouache on illustration board with photo collage pasted.*

Figures 15– 32 and 15-33. *Renderings by Wenhai Ma for* Tartuffe, *by Moliere. The Central Academy of Drama (Beijing), 1984, pen and colored ink on watercolor paper, 12" x 9.5".*

Figures 15-34 through 15-36. *Renderings by Wenhai Ma for* Desire under the Elms *by Eugene O'Neill, the Shenyang Repertory (China), watercolor, gouache over pencil sketch on illustration board, 14""x 10", 1985.*

Figures 15-37 through 15-39. *Renderings by Wenhai Ma for* The Importance of Being Earnest *by Oscar Wilde, Duke University, watercolor, gouache over photo collage. 8 ½" x 11".*

Figure 15-40. *Paint elevation prepared for a drop by Wenhai Ma for* Hamlet *by William Shakespeare, Duke University, 1998, watercolor, India ink on tinted illustration board, 8" x 6 ½".*

Figure 15-41. *Rendering by Wenhai Ma for* Arms and the Man *by George Bernard Shaw, Duke University, 1991, watercolor on paper and Photoshop, 8 ¾" x 6".*

Figure 15-42. *Rendering by Wenhai Ma for* Cymbeline *by William Shakespeare, Duke University, watercolor on paper and Photoshop, 9" x 12 ½", 1991.*

Figure 15-43. *Rendering for* The Three Cuckolds *by Leon Katz. Watercolor and India ink on paper. Duke University, 9 ½" x 6 ½", 1987.*

Figure 15-44. *Rendering by Wenhai Ma for* McTeague *by Frank Norris, colored pencils, gouache on grey pastel paper and Photoshop, 10 ½" x 7 ½". Duke University, 2008.*

Figures 15-45 and 15-46. *Renderings for* Hamlet *by Wenhai Ma, watercolor and India ink, Duke University, 6 ½" x 4 ½" and 20" x 13", 1990.*

Figure 15-47. *Rendering by Wenhai Ma for* The Tempest *by William Shakespeare, watercolor on paper, 7 ½" x 3 ½", 1996.*

Figure 15-48. *Rendering by Wenhai Ma for* The Taming of the Shrew *by William Shakespeare, India ink on watercolor paper, 13 ½" x 11", 1988.*

Figure 15-49. *Rendering by Wenhai Ma for* He Who Gets Slapped, *by David Cairns. 9" x 7.5", 1993, watercolor, India ink on watercolor paper.*

Figure 15-50. *Rendering by Wenhai Ma for* Van Gogh / Gauguin, *watercolor, India ink on watercolor paper, 13" x 10", 1993.*

Figures 15-51 and 15-52. *Renderings by Wenhai Ma for* The House of Blue Leaves *by John Guare. Watercolor, India ink on watercolor paper, 13" x 10", 1993.*

Figure 15-54. *Backdrop elevation by Wenhai Ma for* The Nightingale, *Chapel Hill Ballet Company, 1988. Watercolor, gouache on illustration board.*

Figure 15-53. *Paint elevation by Wenhai Ma for* The Magic Flute, *music by Wolfgang Amadeus Mozart, Durham Arts Council & Triangle Music Theatre Associates, water-soluble pencils over photocopied sketch, 7 ¾" x 5 ½", 1988.*

Figures 15-55 and 15-56. *Renderings by Wenhai Ma for* A Midsummer Night's Dream *by William Shakespeare, the Hong Kong Chung Ying Theater & the Hong Kong Sinfonietta, 2000. Watercolor, gouache over pencil sketch on illustration board, 16″ x 9½″.*

Figures 15-57 and 15-58. *Paint elevations by Wenhai Ma for* Family *by Cao Yu, the Hong Kong Academy for Performing Arts, 2003. Left: watercolor, gouache on illustration board. Right: Oil on canvas board, 20″ x 16″.*

Figure 15-59. *Backdrop elevation by Wenhai Ma for Cantonese Opera* The White Snake, *watercolor on mat board, 6 ¼" x 10 ½", 2004.*

Figure 15-60. *Photoshop-aided rendering by Wenhai Ma for* Falling in Love with Her, *Spring-Time Stage, Hong Kong, 2004,*

Figures 15-61 through 15-63. *Renderings by Wenhai Ma for* No.1 Restaurant in China, *Spring-Time Stage, Hong Kong, 1999, watercolor, India ink and pencil. 16" x 9 ½". 16 ½" x 12 ½".*

Figure 15-64. *Backdrop elevation by Wenhai Ma for* No.1 Restaurant in China, *Spring-Time Stage, Hong Kong, 1999, watercolor and gouache on paper, 10 ½" x 18".*

Figure 15-65. *Poster design by Wenhai Ma for* Turandot, *watercolor, water-soluble pencils, and gouache on illustration board, 2005.*

Figure 15-66. *Rendering by Wenhai Ma for* Crazy Snow, *a musical premiered by the Shanghai Dramatic Center, 2005. Watercolor on paper.*

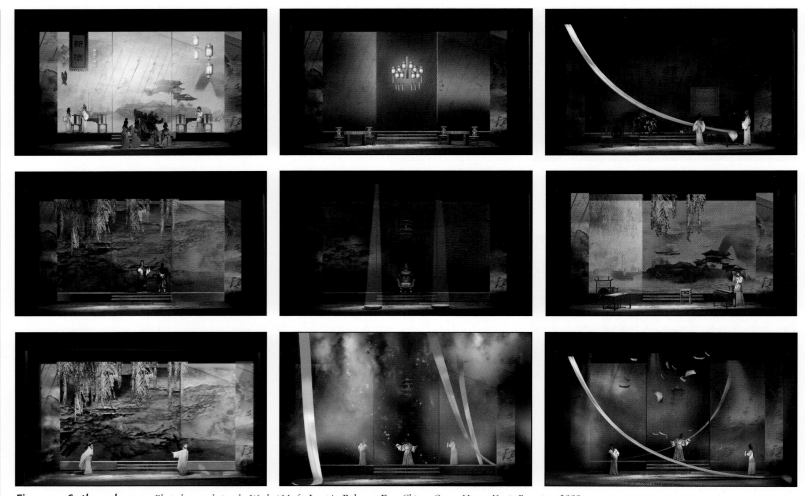

Figures 15-67 through 15-75. *Photoshop renderings by Wenhai Ma for* Lost in Balcony Fog, *Chinese Opera, Hunan Kunju Repertory, 2009.*

 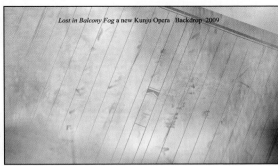

Figures 15-76 through 15-80. *Photoshop renderings by Wenhai Ma for* Lost in Balcony Fog, *Chinese Opera, Hunan Kunju Repertory, 2009.*

Figure 15-81. *Photoshop rendering for* The Magic Flute, *composed by Wolfgang Amadeus Mozart, directed by Kathleen F. Conlin, the University of Illinois at Urbana-Champaign, 2011.*

Figures 15-86 and 15-87. *Costume renderings by Wenhai Ma for* Arms and the Man *by Bernard Shaw. Watercolor, pencil and India ink, 1982, 11" x 8½".*

Figure 15-82. *Rendering by Wenhai Ma for* Moonlight and Valentino, *watercolor on paper, 13" x7½", 1990.*

Figures 15-83 through 15-85. *Costume renderings by Wenhai Ma for* Hamlet *by William Shakespeare. Watercolor and pencil on watercolor paper, 1982, 11" x 8 ½".*

Figures 15- 88 through 15-90. *Costume renderings by Wenhai Ma for* The Imaginary Invalid *by Moliere. Watercolor, gouache on watercolor-tinted paper, 16½" x 11½", 1983.*

Figures 15-91 through 15-95. *Costume renderings by Wenhai Ma for* King Lear *by William Shakespeare, watercolor over charcoal sketch on watercolor paper, 17" x 12½", 1983.*

Figures 15-96 through 15-105. *Costume renderings by Wenhai Ma for* The Winter's Tale, *by William Shakespeare, watercolor, over pencil sketch on watercolor paper, 14" x 11", 1983.*

Figures 15-106 and 15-107. *Costume renderings by Wenhai Ma for* Marco Millions, *by Eugene O'Neill, watercolor over pencil sketch on watercolor paper, 16½" x 11½", 1984.*

Figure 15-108. *Costume rendering by Wenhai Ma for* Mirror, *modern dance, the Hong Kong Academy for Performing Arts, watercolor on paper, 11½" x 16½", 2001.*

Figures 15-109 and 15-110. *Costume renderings by Wenhai Ma for* The Tempest, *by William Shakespeare. Watercolor over pencil sketch, 16½" x 11½", 1982.*

Figures 15-111 through 15-119. *Costume renderings by Wenhai Ma for* Les Contes d'Hoffmann, *music by Jacques Offenbach. Watercolor over pencil sketches, 1983, 24" x 18".*

Figures 15-120 through 15-128. *Costume renderings by Wenhai Ma for* Les Contes d'Hoffmann, *music by Jacques Offenbach. Watercolor over pencil sketches, 1983, 24" x 18".*

Figures 15-129 through 15-136. *Costume renderings by Wenhai Ma for* Les Contes d'Hoffmann, *music by Jacques Offenbach. Watercolor over pencil sketches, 1983, 24″ x 18″.*

Figures 15-141 through 15-146. *Costume renderings by Wenhai Ma for* The Rivals, *by Richard Brinsley Sheridan, watercolor, gouache, pencil on tracing paper, 17" x 11", 1983.*

Figures 15-137 through 15-140. *Costume renderings by Wenhai Ma for* The Winter's Tale, *by William Shakespeare. Watercolor, gouache, ink on rice paper, 10" x 6", 1983.*

Figures 15-147 through 15-150. *Costume renderings by Wenhai Ma for* Duke Bluebeard's Castle, *music by Béla Bartók. Gouache, pencil and markers on paper, 8½" x 11", 1983.*

Figures 15-151 through 15-154. *Costume renderings by Wenhai Ma for* Tartuffe *by Moliere. Watercolor and India ink. The Central Academy of Drama (Beijing), 1983.*

Figures 15-155 through 15-158. *Costume renderings by Wenhai Ma for* The Barber of Seville, *music by Wolfgang Amadeus Mozart. Watercolor on paper, the Hong Kong Academy for Performing Arts, 17″ x 11″, 1998.*

Figures 15-159, 160 and 15-161. *Costume renderings by Wenhai Ma for* The Father *by August Strindberg. Gouache and pencil on paper, Duke University, 17″ x 11″, 1997.*

Figures 15-162 through 15-165. *Illustrations by Wenhai Ma for* Monkey King Defeats Red Boy, *Pan Asian Publications, USA, 2009. Watercolor and India ink, 21" x 14".*

Student Work

The following renderings were done by the students I taught in my Rendering and Designer Media classes. Their permissions and support are greatly appreciated.

Figure 15-166. *Rendering by Steve Barnes for* Road *by Jim Cartwright, directed by Richard Stockton Rand, Purdue University. Watercolor, ink and pencil on paper, 8½" x 11", 2005.*

Figure 15-167. *Rendering by DeAnne Kennedy for* Vertical Window, *a practice in Scene Design based on two words provided by the instructor, R. Eric Stone; watercolor, ink and pencil on paper, 8½" x 11", 2008.*

Figure 15-168. *Rendering by Sarah E. Ross for* Fugitive Kind *by Tennessee Williams, directed by Tom Mitchell, the University of Illinois at Urbana-Champaign. Watercolor, and India ink on paper, 9" x 12", 2009.*

Figure 15-169. *Rendering by Tara A. Houston for* Romeo et Juliette, *music by Charles Gounod, libretto by Jules Barbier and Michel Carré, University of Illinois at Urbana-Champaign, watercolor, and India ink on paper, 2008.*

Figure 15-170. *Rendering by Stephanie Polhemus for* Armide, *by Jean-Baptiste Lully, directed by James Zager, the University of Illinois at Urbana-Champaign, watercolor on paper, 11" x 17", 2008.*

Figure 15-171. *Rendering by Jenna Engelmann for* Necessary Targets, *by Eve Ensler, directed by Linda Gillum, the University of Illinois at Urbana-Champaign, watercolor on paper, 11" x 17", 2009.*

Figure 15-172. *In the Woods, rendering by Moon Jung Kim, a practice in Rendering class based on pencil cartoon provided by the instructor, Wenhai Ma, watercolor and gouache on illustration board, 11" x 16", 2003-08.*

Figures 15-173-175. *Students' class projects. Left to right:* **Miss Julie,** *by August Strindberg, rendering by Yu Su, pencil and watercolor on paper, 10" x 15", 2011;* **The Miser** *by Moliere, rendering by Amanda Williams, Photoshop over pencil sketch, 2011;* **Miss Julie,** *rendering by Kevin Grab, pencil and watercolor on paper, 2011.*

About the Author

Wenhai Ma
www.ma.vecface.com

Photo by Valerie A. Oliveiro

Wenhai Ma received his BFA in Scene Design from the Central Academy of Drama (Beijing) and MFA in Scene & Costume Design from Carnegie Mellon University. Before he joined the Department of Theatre and chairing the Scene Design Program at the University of Illinois at Urbana-Champaign, he had taught at the University of Nebraska-Lincoln, Purdue University, the Hong Kong Academy for Performing Arts, Duke University, and the Central Academy of Drama (Beijing), respectively. He has designed sets and costumes in the US and Asia, including sets for *Watership Down* (Lifeline, Chicago), *The Magic Flute* (University of Illinois at Urbana-Champaign), *College Widow* (Purdue University), *The Peach Blossom Valley*, set and costumes (Changde Han Opera Repertory, China), *Crazy Snow* (Shanghai Drama Center), *Turandot* (Opera Hong Kong), *Moonlight and Valentino* (Pre-Broadway), *Macbeth, Arsenic and Old Lace* (Duke Stage Company), *Widows* (Hip Pocket Theatre, Texas), *How I Learned Driving* (Man Bites Dog Theatre, North Carolina), *The Greeks* (Carnegie Mellon). He has been invited as guest lecturer to conduct workshops and seminars by universities and institutions. He has also illustrated picture books for publishers such as Morrow Junior, Viking, Pan Asian Publications (USA) and Candlewick. Professor Ma has conducted lots of theatre rendering and watercolor workshops for many institutions and groups including at the 50th United States Institute for Theatre Technology Annual Conference. He has recently moved to Singapore and is teaching at the Nanyang Academy of Fine Arts.

Credits

Figure 2-34: Manhattan Skyscrapers from below. @Nikada, iStock Photo

Figure 2-46: Leonardo da Vinci (1452-1519), *Mona Lisa*, c. 1503-6 (oil on panel). Louvre, Paris, France / Giraudon / The Bridgeman Art Library International.

Figure 2-52: Joseph Mallord William Turner (1775-1851), *The Red Rigi*, 1842 (watercolor on paper). National Gallery of Victoria, Melbourne, Australia / Felton Bequest / The Bridgeman Art Library International.

Figure 3-1: Rembrandt van Rijn (1606-69), *The Nightwatch*, c. 1642 (oil on canvas). Rijksmuseum, Amsterdam, The Netherlands / The Bridgeman Art Library International.

Figure 5-1: Paul Sandby (1725-1809), *Chepstow Castle*, (watercolor). Private Collection / Photo © Agnew's, London, UK / The Bridgeman Art Library International.

Figure 9-1: Anders Leonard Zorn (1860-1920), *En premïar (Her First Dip)*. Atkinson Art Gallery, Southport, Lancashire, UK / The Bridgeman Art Library International.